The Beauty and Vanity of Denial

Start to Finish books may be purchased upon request.
Email: contact@denialanddepression.com

The first, Start to Finish paperback edition published 2016
Printed in the United States of America.

Cover Design
"Angel Wooden Queen"
By Joffrey Pavesi
www.facebook.com/JPavesiarts
E-mail: hannibawl@gmail.com

The Library of Congress has catalogued the paperback edition as follows:

Taylor, Angela, 1966-
The Beauty and Vanity of Denial: Unmask Your Stories and Embrace Your Truth/
By Angela Taylor

The Beauty and Vanity of Denial

Unmask Your Stories and Embrace Your Truth

Angela Taylor

TABLE OF CONTENTS

The
Beauty and Vanity
of Denial:

Unmask Your Stories
And Embrace Your Truth

Angela Taylor

Dedication

This book is dedicated to my dad
for being in my life
when I needed him the most.
I miss you.

Acknowledgements

I am thankful to both my mom and sister, Donarae, for being a listening ear to let me know I was moving in the right direction.

I also want to thank all of those who helped to bring this book into manifestation through their loving support, hard work, and patience during the process of writing, editing, and re-editing. A special thanks goes out to Walter Beckley, my publisher for his literary insight; Finisha O'Quinn and Kim Burger, my editors for their patience, expertise, and due diligence. In addition, Joffrey Pavesi for the cover image. You have equally helped to make my dream a reality.

I also want to thank my tenth grade English teacher, Mrs. Beverly, for encouraging me to continue writing when I didn't have much confidence in my writing ability or myself. Your encouragement made a huge impact on me and I will be forever grateful!

Praise for *The Beauty and Vanity of Denial*

Angela's writing stirs my soul in ways that I haven't felt before. Her words are like a jazzman improvising solo on a tenor saxophone in a smoky nightclub on a Saturday night and a deep sermon on the mount on Sunday morning. She takes you to places emotionally you never knew existed before. She makes you long to continue reading or listening within, when the last note of the night has been played, which is like the period at the end of the last sentence telling you the chapter or book is over. She paints beautiful pictures with her words that opens the door of your imagination and invites the images she creates with her pen to come to life and perform in the theatre of your mind. Her writings pull you into a world you may not be familiar with, but find fascinating, as you learn about a world outside of your own, however somehow, you've been involved with your entire life.

Walter L. Beckley- Author, *Breathe in God's Love & Light*

If you have ever felt like life has you treading water in an ocean comprised of waves of denial, Angela's book is the life preserver pulling you back to shore to discover the land you lost.

For me, battling Bipolar I disorder has had me experiencing everything Angela has (and more), but her book helped me find my Truths and bury Deny into the ground, six feet under. This book was written to help those of us searching for a way to fight our past and enlighten our future.

Kim Burger- Editor

"For a man to conquer himself is the first and noblest of all victories."
~ Plato

Personal Overview

I have always been curious about human nature— why do we behave the way we do; how do we end up in the various good and not-so-good situations and circumstances we live with; and why do some people seem to have it all together and others seem to be barely holding on? I usually had questions after any interaction I experienced, but most times I could not come up with an answer or my own answers, which were sophomoric at best, were based on the very limited knowledge and understanding I had about myself or other people and life in general.

These questions have always been with me as I accumulated and assimilated happy and hurtful experiences year after year. Life generated more questions for my mind to ponder, which left me to believe that my brain is a three-pound magnet that attracts my personal, mental, emotional, and even physical inquiries, insults, and illusions about others and me. My denial ran deeper than the Nile—with the help of my own magnetic field.

My answers came later in life when I felt like my world was falling apart. I needed answers to my questions immediately, as I was slowly turning into a person I didn't want to be. My answers may not be your answers; however, they may be just what you have been searching for.

This book is about my experiences as I navigated my life, looking for an escape route that would lead to my freedom from sadness, anger, doubt, and fear. Fortunately, I had to experience all that I had to come to the point where I felt like it was now or never. Something needed to change; I found that something to be me.

Most of the time we look outside ourselves for answers. We look for things that will cover up, bury, and hide what we see in the mirror or encounter from the outside world, what we feel when we wake up in the morning, what we hear from the people in our inner and even outer circle, and what we desire to taste, feel, see, or understand. Yet, in settling, somehow we've learned how to make do with the less attractive alternative. It is as if what we smell in our environment that makes us wrinkle our nose or what we reach out to touch that never reaches back, makes us stop trying to achieve and instead accept what we have already obtained and deny wanting something more.

Discovering the distinction between what you accept versus what you really want is an important step. This step will lead to understanding the story that has been told by you in order to accept your current situation, instead of going after your true desire(s).

I found the one thing holding me back and impeding my freedom was my denial stories. We all make decisions based on our perceptions and what we believe we want or need at a given moment. I am no exception. I believe that most of us move past where we are in various areas of our lives to a different stage in which what we wanted, or needed before, no longer applies. There are also times when we are forced to change due to outside circumstances, yet, instead of accepting the change within us and allowing the change to occur outside of our sphere of influence, we make excuses. We justify why we should continue the same path, knowing something has changed or has to change, in order to realize our dreams. Sometimes the things that no longer fit are people, relationships, financial situations, or career and lifestyle choices. In addition, attitudes, old perspectives, religious ideologies, biases, old habits and behaviors, emotional immaturity, and activities we engage in may no longer be appropriate for us.

I discovered I used denial stories to make myself feel better and to hide behind when I didn't want to face something emotionally painful. I used denials to hide my personal issues that I didn't want to acknowledge or to continue blaming everyone else for my circumstances. I used denials to hide feelings of inadequacy, loneliness, and rejection. Before I discovered them, my denial stories kept me from moving forward with my life in the areas where they were dominating my thoughts and controlling my actions until I acknowledged them, examined them, and began to unravel them to find the reasons why they were in play. Although I have moved through some denials and am in a better place physically, mentally, and emotionally, I still find myself falling back into old habits, though now I can see it immediately, laugh at myself, and see my truth even when it's uncomfortable to face. That's a stark contrast to how I handled challenges before I uncovered my first denial story.

I feel like I have had a breakthrough and want to share my insight, the method I used to overcome the trance my denials kept me in, and my liberation. My hope is that what I have learned on my journey, will assist you in restoring your body, mind, and life to optimal health so you can begin to enjoy areas of your life that, presently, leave you feeling frustrated, angry, and exhausted.

If overcoming denial helped me, perhaps it will help you, too. Keep reading and answer the questions that are listed in order for you to begin to overcome your denials and reveal the hidden opportunities that are open to you.

My Hiding Place: Poem

I see them, even in the dark spinning around
In slow motion and up into a spiral
Like a giant tornado in miniature.
They are whirling around inside a water bottle cap
Dropped by mom as it slipped through her fingers
And into the coffee cup which is immersed in water
Surrounded by marbles at the bottom of the vase,
Enclosed with green wrapping paper and tin foil
Stuffed with pink and purple cotton.
The vase is at the bottom of a toy chest filled with dusty,
Broken toys that sits on top of a trunk behind the rocking
chair covered with grandma's
Blue and white polka dot quilt that has a large brown
Photo album in its seat filled with black and white faded
Pictures and pressed flowers from proms, graduations,
Birthday parties, and Valentine's Day roses
Long dead, with a smell of mildew and plastic from the

Clear film holding the pictures in place.
The rocking chair creaks as it moves in the attic behind
The sewing machine with the rickety table that
Grandma had to prop up with a book.
The table is sitting next to the shoe boxes speckled with
Black shoe polish and filled with thread, thimbles,
Measuring tape, needles, straight pins, and safety pins—
Most of her utensils used for sewing.
The shoe boxes are against the wall close to the broken
Window that has been painted shut for years by dad so
Long ago. The window is near the stairs where the old
Blankets spotted with dirt, wine stains, and bread
Crumbs still clinging to the knots in the fabric are lying
On top of the tan wicker picnic basket we took to the
Park, filled with potato salad, fried chicken, homemade
Rolls, chocolate cake, and lemonade.

They are in constant motion, but hidden from view
Far away from prying eyes and ears listening, trying but
Failing to hear a distant instrument
Still playing down through the years.
I can hear it, but they can't. The sound waves hanging in
The air left behind from the stories, the lies, the hurt and

Pain that sometimes lingers

Even after they have been removed from view.

That is where I hide them. That is where they stay.

That is where they taunt me,

Poke me, prod me, and push me.

I deny their existence. I deny they are a part of me.

I deny that they make me do things

I wish I didn't, that others can see.

No matter how fast the momentum quickens,

I will never let them out. It doesn't matter how loud they

Get, or how much energy it takes

To keep them concealed. I'll go down fighting to keep

Them hidden until the very end.

- Angela Taylor

"Everything we hear is an opinion, not a fact.
Everything we see is a perspective,
not the truth."
- Marcus Aurelius

To My Readers

My book is one perspective among multitudes. I am writing this book because of my desire to help as many people as I can who could be living in denial (like I was and am still at times), and may not know it. Perhaps you are experiencing signs of denial, which may include challenges with: losing weight; managing and saving money; initiating, creating and developing healthy friendships and love relationships; feeling good naturally; having unlimited energy; sleeping well; thinking clearly; or extreme emotional highs and lows. What you are experiencing may also be indications of stress. These could be frequent headaches, hair breakage, upset stomach, acid reflux, or anxiety attacks. They may also include signs of depression that may be exacerbated by stress such as prolonged periods of sadness, emptiness, or mental and emotional fatigue. These are all signs and symptoms I endured while living my life in denial. I did not know why I had them at the time, but now I can see a connection between my denials and their physical and psychological manifestation in every area of my life.

I am writing a book about denial because I discovered at the very root of the sadness, frustration, and anger I felt when diagnosed with depression was denial of what I truly thought and felt about the life I was living and its stark contrast to the life I wanted for myself. I found that I was in denial about many things in different areas of my life. I will list the "8 Areas of the Circle of Life," introduced to me by Walter L. Beckley, author of the book, *Breathe in God's Love & Light,* as we take a closer look at how denial can reveal itself in various areas of our lives.

Although I am writing about my experience directly before and after being diagnosed with depression, this book will be about the denials that led to my diagnosis. You will read all about the beauty and vanity of depression in a future book.

The denials I carried with me from childhood into adulthood, and those accumulating through the years intensified by stress, led to my diagnosis of depression and anxiety. They also however, led to a transformation in my thoughts, attitudes, behaviors, and expectations.

This ultimately caused an awareness I did not have before and an attainment of a new life. My new life has a feeling of freedom and authenticity it did not have before. Once I acknowledged my denials, I recognized I needed to make some changes. I began taking the necessary steps leading to the changes that I wanted. The inspiration and guidance I received during this time released the joy and uncovered the peace of mind I had not felt for several years.

There were many days during this time in my life that I wondered what was wrong with me. On one occasion, I decided I wanted to determine why I was not enjoying my life. I was discontented with feeling bad; I wanted to feel good. I needed something to change quickly!

Still in the middle of the biggest challenge I had in my life up to that point and feeling its signs and symptoms, I began to ask questions that I was then brave enough to answer truthfully. During this self-analysis, I realized that my mind and body were experiencing turmoil because of what I thought and how I felt about my life. I also began to understand what I thought and how I felt about my life was an extension of what I thought and how I felt about myself. I knew that I had shortcomings that I needed to work on, but blamed others and saw myself as a victim in all of the scenarios in my mind.

I discovered, while observing my thoughts and emotions, a pattern had developed. I had in the past monitored my conscious thoughts, but had not considered my unconscious thoughts nor considered the emotions connected to the stories I repeated in my head. These are the stories that are on a loop in our mind that we disregard because we believe it is harmless chatter. It is not harmless chatter. These thoughts are sometimes filled with denials responsible for many of the challenges we have. My lack of awareness and, or indifference to the chatter is the reason I kept ending up in the same situations and feeling the same emotions throughout my life. This dialogue had not changed in forty plus years. There were many denials embedded in these stories that, up until that point, had made it impossible for me to break free from the negative emotions I felt.

I started monitoring my thoughts when I decided I desperately wanted to change my life. I knew the adage "we are what we eat," but we are also what we think and what we feel. I realized at that time I thought about the same situations, conversations, and events each and every day. It felt as if they were haunting me. I found the narrative had negative energy or emotions attached that were responsible for much of my feelings, both mentally and physically. Before this, I had only monitored my conscious thoughts for negativity. I had not considered how this passive, yet active, repetitive, free-flowing, unsupervised part of my psyche had my mind and emotions in a constant state of flux, with a mix of denials at the root of it all. I had thought about these same scenarios so often they became my constant dialogue. I only noticed them during my down times when my mind was not busy working on something in the present and they could resurface, keeping me in limbo. These thoughts and emotions had become automatic; I had uncovered a default setting to which my mind always returned. This pattern took the form of recurring thoughts and emotions about the same situations, conversations, circumstances, experiences, and people resulting in a negative impact on my psyche. Included in these scenarios were the denials underlying each one and the conscious decisions I made in an effort to hide the truth and protect myself.

I discovered there were areas of my life I had decided certain topics of conversation would not be initiated or discussed because avoiding them allowed me to feel safe, secure, and loved. Denying my truth in order to feel these things, which were so important to me, made the emotional chaos worthwhile for a period of time, until suppressing it became unbearable.

Maybe you have not had the time or felt you had a reason to take a closer look at why you make the decisions you do and how they have affected your life. This book may have shown up at the right time for you to start to investigate why certain things are happening in your life—repeatedly. It is also possible, for now, you just want a bit of information and you are not ready to move toward change yet. That is ok, too.

It is my aim to generate questions in your mind that compel you to examine your thoughts about every area of your life. I want you to especially pay attention to areas you believe could use some improvement. After developing insight into your own psyche, maybe you will decide to initiate changes that will result in living the life you have always wanted, or at the very least, feeling better about your life while living it.

In my conversations with other individuals, women, in particular, I have found there are many of us who are living in denial, which has led to depression and we have not realized it. There are also many of us who know that living in denial is affecting someone we love, but don't know what we can do to help them. I hope you find some answers in this book.

I want to help you stop the cycle of confusion, discomfort, frustration, anxiety, complacency, and sometimes hopelessness that comes from living with denial stories controlling your every move. I want to create a movement for change. I want you to feel better, be well, enjoy your life, and have peace of mind as a byproduct! I want you to live the life you have always wanted, but wasn't sure if it was possible for you!

There are many of us who know something is wrong and do not know what it is or what to do about it. There are some of us who know what is wrong, but are afraid to look too closely because of the emotional pain involved. As you will learn later in the book, it is not harmful to deny for a short period of time, as this can give your psyche a chance to absorb the information or event that may have been very painful or shocking to you in that moment. However, it is important for you to eventually move through this period of denial into acceptance and be free to take advantage of opportunities waiting for you to get yourself back into the flow of life.

Before I decided to inspect my life, I felt as if I was going around in circles. I knew there were issues in my life that needed to be addressed, but I thought other people caused my challenges. I didn't realize my challenges had everything to do with me. I refused to look at the issues keeping me tied down; it was as if I was in a chamber with one hole to breathe through. I was suffering and it was because I didn't want to change yet. I didn't want to deal with the transformations that would inevitably occur once I decided to look my challenges square in the face and feel the emotions connected to them. I was happy to live with my denial stories; they served me well, for quite a while, until I began to feel trapped by them; incarcerated by my own mind...willingly. That is insanity...voluntarily staying in denial because I thought it was better than the alternative, even though I was suffering. How much worse could the alternative have been? It wasn't; I just wasn't ready to change, yet.

I was comfortable in my denial stories, but they kept me in one place, unable to move forward and missing out on opportunities because my mind was in turmoil. I will give you an example: While I was deep in denial and depression, I applied for a job and went to the interview. I kept telling myself consciously that it was ok, that I needed the job and it was just what I had been looking for. I went to the job interview, but found myself saying and doing things that were inappropriate, such as giving the manager a hug and a back slap. When I did it, I wondered why. I had never done that before to anyone in my life. That's what men usually do when greeting their male friends and I am not a male nor was he my friend. He was a potential manager and this was the greeting before an interview for a position with his company. It went downhill from there. I knew that I shouldn't have applied for the job. I knew that I shouldn't have accepted the interview. I knew that I shouldn't have been there. I knew that I wasn't ready to take that position at that time. I knew all of this before I even applied, but instead of accepting my truth (that I was depressed and not mentally or emotionally ready to handle the responsibilities that came with the position), I decided it was a good opportunity and too hard to pass up, no matter how I felt. Yes, it was a great opportunity, if I had been ready for it. It would have been perfect. It was exactly what I thought I wanted and I was the kind of employee they were looking for at the time. However, I wasn't ready and I knew it. I denied the reality in favor of the story (I can't pass this opportunity up. I have to go for it). We went through the interview as if all was well. I had the qualifications they were seeking, but I knew after that hug I gave him he said to himself, "That was strange. I'm not sure about her." He spoke to me as if I had the job, but said he needed to speak with his manager first. I never heard from him after that and I never reached out to inquire as to why he didn't call me. I knew. I had blown it. I wasn't ready for the position. I didn't even really want it at that point. I had been pushing myself very hard for a very long time. I needed to rest. As you will learn later in the book, that is a recurring theme in my life. I say "yes" to more responsibility when I really need to say "no, thanks" and run away. That was a missed opportunity that could have worked out well if I had been ready to handle it. I wasn't ready and I was in denial about being ready.

You may be experiencing the same feelings of being on a merry-go-round and wanting to get off. You may be saying yes, when you really want to say no to people, food, more responsibilities, invitations to places you don't need to be, sex, drugs, over-time, etc., but don't because of the denial story in your head. Perhaps this book can help you overcome your denial so you are ready and available for the opportunities awaiting your return to authenticity, sanity/mental health, clarity, rationality, etc. You get the message.

I believe we all go through challenges in life in order to become wiser and it is our responsibility to help someone else who may be having the same challenges. We become wiser by learning from our experiences how to be more aware of, and sensitive to, our intuition (our internal guidance system) and complying with it.

It's important to apply whatever we learn to our lives and then teach someone else what we've learned and how to apply it to their lives. I also believe we experience certain situations and live under certain circumstances so we can eventually wake up, peel back the layers of denial, acknowledge our truth, and begin to move through the obstacles that come with the challenges we all have. I am repeating this again because it is important to remember. I believe when we work through the challenges and are better for it, it is our responsibility to reach out and take the hand of someone else and say, "Come with me, I'll show you how I made it through. Perhaps what I went through will help you make it through, too."

This book gives voice to what I've experienced in my life as a person just like you. I lived day-to-day, yet felt dissatisfied with my relationships, my life, and myself. I'm writing this book because, even though I am still learning, no one can tell me that my life is not a direct result of my thoughts, feelings, actions, and expectations. I pushed myself to the point that I felt like it was now or never. I had to take a step in what I knew was the right direction and deal with the collateral damage, one day at a time, in order for me to get back to living a life that felt authentic; a life where I didn't have to hide my emotions and thoughts because of fear.

When I decided to focus on how I wanted to be and the kind of relationships I wanted in my life, I had to change. I decided to be the kind of person that I want a relationship with. I stopped blaming and began taking responsibility for my life. As I began to acknowledge my truth, I began to act and react differently to the situations, circumstances, and people around me. I began to focus on what I wanted and enjoyed instead of what I didn't like and didn't enjoy. Soon, what I began to see was what I focused on became what I experienced.

The more I listened to my truth, the more I began to feel like anything was possible. The more I listened to my truth, the better I began to feel...mixed with a little apprehension, but ten times better. That is when I began to feel free. That is when I began taking steps leading toward the life I really wanted. That is when my life began to change.

Some of you may know you are living in denial and want to move beyond it, so you can feel better, be better, and live better. This book will give insight into some of my experiences with denial—what denial is, how to detect it, what it may look and feel like in the various areas of your life, challenges you may go through as a result, and what you can do to begin to get your thoughts, emotions, and life back on track.

It is my prayer that if the information contained in this book resonates with you, you will answer the questions I pose and become aware of the true answers (nobody else has to know but you at this point). When you feel brave enough to begin making moves you believe will lead to living a better life and experiencing greater opportunities, take the first step. Remember, just because you have obstacles placed, blown, thrown, kicked, or dropped in your path, does not mean you should stop. We all have to go through some challenges to make it to where we want to be. Change is going to require modifications in you. If you are ready to change, keep reading.

I want to define a few terms that I will mention in the book so that what I am writing about is clear.

True, as I am using it, means being the case rather than what is manifested or assumed.

Truth can be: sincerity in action, character, and utterance; the state of being the case: fact; the body of real things, events, and facts: actuality; a transcendent fundamental or spiritual reality; *capitalized* Christian Science: god.

Your truth is what you believe is right or best for you. Your truth is based solely on your perception of what will lead to a life that feels authentic to you.

When I write about Truth, I am writing about our higher self, super consciousness, or spiritual self.

You will see authentic mentioned many times. **Authentic** is a synonym of genuine, which is a definition of honest.

Honest is defined as not hiding the truth about someone or something: not meant to deceive someone;

free from fraud or deception: legitimate, truthful: genuine, real.

Authentic, as I am using it, is defined as: true to one's own personality, spirit, or character (Merriam Webster Dictionary).

I want to mention that, if done long enough, something we may label "bad" can feel authentic to us. For example, we can create bad habits such as speaking a certain way (cursing), lying and behaving in ways not beneficial to our health, relationships, financial stability, career advancement, lifestyle, progress, freedom, etc.   We can abuse ourselves and even provoke others to abuse us because of a cycle of abuse we have been conditioned to expect and accept over a period of time; it can begin to feel natural.   Although these behaviors may feel authentic, they cause chaos and pain in our lives and possibly the lives of others. They may also stagnate our growth and the restoration process.

When you see **authentic** in this book, what I mean is: being true to your best and most honorable self, defined in Webster as, characterized by integrity.

Thank you for purchasing my book. Let me know when you begin to see changes in yourself and your life. I'm interested to know how it works for you. Peace and love, now and forever.

Epitome of Denial: Poem

I'm fine
I'm Ok...
Lost the house, the economy is bad
Lost the car, couldn't afford to pay the note
Lost the kids, fool lied and said I was a bad mom
Lost my mind, worrying about the bills
Lost my money, at the boat
Lost my pride, begging him to come back
Lost my dog, ran away
Lost my cat, left with the dog
Lost my job, couldn't get up on time
Lost my health, I like junk food and hate exercise
Lost my reason, stay in bed most of the day
But, I'm Ok... Can I get a loan?

                         - Angela Taylor

"By three methods we may learn wisdom: first, by reflection which is noblest; second, by imitation, which is the easiest; and third, by experience, which is the bitterest."
- Confucius

Denial Introduction

The Merriam-Webster Dictionary defines denial, as I am using it for this book, as, "A psychological defense mechanism in which confrontation with a personal problem or with reality is avoided by <u>denying the existence</u> of the problem or reality.

In denial, is defined as <u>refusing to admit</u> the truth or reality of something unpleasant. Some of the synonyms that are appropriate are non-acceptance and refusal.

Additional synonyms of denial are: rejection, disallowance, declination, withholding, forbidding, no, negation, and disapproval (abcthesaurus.com).

A denial can be used as a tool to help you move through the grieving process. It can be used as a long-term method to help you hide or reinvent the truth. It can be used to make you feel better during tough times or to make you feel superior to other individuals or groups of people. It can be used to maintain the status quo and can be socially acceptable, therefore, giving you permission for its continuance. It can be used to acquire something you want by helping you ignore the situations or circumstances you are in and do not want. It can be used to help you maintain your relationships. It can be used as an excuse to not change or take action. It can be used to boost your ego. It can also be used to bury past experiences. Finally, it can be used as a statement rejecting an appearance that you do not want.

The Stress of Denial

Living in denial of my truths led to mental, emotional, and physical stress. As mentioned earlier in the book, I lived in denial for decades. As I approached my forties, I began feeling anxious because I had not accomplished all I had wanted to by that time. I was over 25 when I found what I thought was my calling...to have a career as a professional fitness instructor and personal trainer. From the first day I began teaching fitness classes, I loved it. My first involvement with teaching came after I took a group exercise instructors course at Chicago

State University. I had never thought about teaching fitness classes until my sister suggested it to me. She and I enjoyed walking along Chicago's Lake Michigan shoreline and I had always been pretty active. My two favorite activities at that time were walking and dancing. When she mentioned it, my interest was piqued. I decided to find out more about it. I found an instructors class that taught students the fundamentals of creating, organizing, planning, and conducting fitness classes. Needless to say, I really enjoyed it.

I wanted to practice my skills, see if I would enjoy teaching and find out if the classes I had created would be well received. At that time, there were not any hybrid combo classes like what my class became known as— Cardio Jam, a combination of various styles of dance and calisthenics with some light stretching to end the class.

I decided to volunteer first to test the waters, so to speak. I volunteered to teach at the South Side YMCA in Chicago. I had practiced my routines before my first class for several hours a day, for a few weeks. I wasn't nervous because I made sure I practiced often enough to know what I was doing. I was a little apprehensive since I wanted the class to flow the way I had envisioned it, as well as be a fun and pleasant time for the members. Well, I enjoyed that first class beyond measure and the members seemed to like it, too. A new fitness instructor was born!

After a couple of years of learning and teaching many fitness class modalities at health club facilities in the Chicago area, I wanted to learn more. I decided to study and earn a national certification as a personal trainer. I accomplished this, but that wasn't enough. I didn't feel like I knew enough to really be effective. I needed more practical knowledge, so I found a school in the city, The University of Illinois at Chicago, that offered a kinesiology program and I enrolled. This is when the stress I felt began to compound with each new activity or responsibility I added to my already hectic life.

I started my career very late. I was in my thirties by that time and had been married for years, so I had responsibilities the average college student did not have. Within the first year of pursuing my degree, I decided I wanted to start a family. I was getting close to forty and felt like it was now or never. We were not able to conceive, so I began fertility treatments. Because I was over thirty-five, I was considered a high risk, so my doctor wanted me to curb my activities, but how could I curb my activities when I was teaching and taking classes in which I had to be active? That situation led to more stress. I didn't want to, but I stopped teaching fitness classes and informed my college instructors about my doctor's concerns. They understood and were very accommodating. That was a relief, but not completely because I felt as if I wasn't going to get the full impact of my educational classes. Learning practical skills is the reason I had enrolled in the first place, but I gave my frustration to Deny to hide away for a while, until my circumstances changed. You will find out more about Deny later.

I attended all of my classes that semester and started the process of in-vitro fertilization. That was no small undertaking; at one point it seemed as if I had a doctor's appointment every other day. Then I had to begin injecting myself with hormones and I was not a fan of needles hence, to do it myself, well, needless to say, my stress level went up a couple of more notches. Even though my husband and I adhered to all that was required, we didn't conceive. I was devastated and he was disappointed because we had both had our hopes up. I cried some and then went on with life as usual— minus the doctor visits and shots. I had put that behind me, or so I thought. I had to continue working through school and maintaining the household as best I could in my less than optimal mental and emotional state. I didn't realize it at the time, but the stress of trying to conceive while taking college classes (with all that it entails) in addition to maintaining a household was more stressful than I wanted to admit. "I can handle it all. I'm strong!" That is what I told myself. Well, I was so strong (I thought) that I began trying to get back into exercising again. This proved to be very difficult after having not exercised for months. The disappointment of not conceiving had affected our marital relationship, but neither of us talked about it. I was definitely in denial and it was too painful to consider other options for becoming parents at the time. In addition, I had put all of my efforts into doing well in school.

My housework began to drop down a few notches on my priority list because I was usually studying, doing homework, writing papers, or working on some big project that was worth half of my grade in the class. This lack of time and energy didn't go unnoticed. I could hear a voice in the back of my mind whisper every now and then saying something like, "Did you put the clothes in the dryer this morning?" or "There are no clean forks or plates left and the kitchen floor is sticky in front of the refrigerator from when you spilled the juice two days ago." This added to my stress level. In addition to that, I didn't have the time or energy to cook meals regularly, not that I cooked every day to begin with, but more often than I had at this time. I would get a phone call from my husband and when he asked what was for dinner, my reply would be, "I don't know. Can you pick up something?" After a while I would hear, "I'm tired of eating restaurant food." I couldn't blame him. He was working two jobs and didn't want to have to come home and cook. I didn't want him to either, but what was I supposed to do? I began to cook dinner for us at least three times a week. I don't know how consistent I was, but I did make an effort.

I then began training clients in my studio, started a walking group, participated in walk-a-thons for charity, and joined a new church and became a member of the choir. If that wasn't enough, I started teaching fitness classes at the university's recreation facility and at church. Then to add insult to injury, I became the coordinator for the Wellness Ministry at church. To be honest, I had only wanted to become a member, but the group needed leadership and since I was in the health and fitness industry, I thought whom best than me. I knew deep inside that it was not a good idea for me to try to tackle another project, with everything else I had going on. However, it seemed like an opportunity I couldn't pass up, so I took it...more denial.

I was so stressed out, I noticed while sitting under the hair dryer at the salon one afternoon that my legs were shaking. I tried to make them stop, but even after breathing deeply and attempting to relax, I couldn't. I was amazed. I had no idea that my body was being affected in this way.

In addition to all of my extra-curricular activities, my relationships were in need of considerable repair...all of them. I had developed some other stress related signs and symptoms which are listed in the book, but the shaking of my legs was surprising because I had fooled myself into thinking I had everything under control. I didn't. I had developed a chronic cough, which turned out to be acid reflux. My hair was breaking off in certain areas of my scalp and right before I decided to see a psychologist, I had started having anxiety attacks. These caused me to feel heart palpitations, labored breathing, and at times, crying spells. I had no control over the duration. The only thing I could do was ride it out until that emotion or energy had been released.

From Stress to Anxiety

The anxiety attacks began after watching a horror movie (I love horror movies, especially with zombies). It was an excellent movie. I remember that while I was watching, I had to continue to tell myself to relax because I could feel my heart starting to race. At the end of the movie, tears began rolling down my face and I couldn't understand why. I wasn't sad. I thought, "This is weird. I can't stop crying." Then I felt my heart racing and couldn't catch my breath. I had to think about something else before I was able to get a handle on it and calm down, but it took a few minutes.

After that incident, I noticed I couldn't multi-task, especially while driving. Before the anxiety attacks, I would be able to drive and talk on the phone (while using my hands free device, of course), listen to the radio, and eat—all at the same time. Now, I couldn't talk on the phone, listen to the radio, or eat while driving. I could only focus on driving. This was a new adventure for me.

I was amazed at how limited my cognitive abilities had become. I was even more amazed and intrigued by how the human brain works. My adventure didn't stop there. I noticed that when I drove over any bridge, I would feel extremely anxious and could not look to either side of me. I could only look directly ahead. I tried to look over the side of a bridge once while driving, and had to pull over and stop my car until my heart slowed and returned back to normal. I had never experienced anything remotely like that before in my life. Now, every once in a while, if I feel stressed and don't realize it, I feel anxiety. It causes me to be overwhelmed. When I feel that way, I know it is time to slow down, delegate, or take something off of my plate.

I felt a certain way about having to slow down, but now I just say, "It is what it is." I make an effort not to worry about something I can do nothing about. I would beat myself up about it, but I have learned to be more kind to myself. I still get frustrated at times because I want to push myself like I used to. After pushing myself so hard for so long, it has been a very challenging habit to break. I have had to realize I am not that person anymore and I don't need to do that to accomplish what I think I need to, nor do I need to accomplish everything in one day. It has been a big adjustment to find balance in all that I do and it is a work in progress.

From Anxiety to Depression

I was diagnosed with depression right after I began having anxiety attacks. If I didn't want to admit something was wrong before, I had to admit it after the first attack. There was no denying what happened, and I had a witness to the first attack who encouraged me to talk with a therapist. After being diagnosed with depression, my therapist told me I didn't look depressed. She said I looked good for someone who was depressed. I told her that I hid it well, which was the truth. I had a lot of practice, but my mental, emotional, and physical well-being were in serious jeopardy.

There were times when I would feel absolutely empty like I had nothing left. I couldn't feel anything. I didn't want to do anything. I could only interact with close friends and family since interacting with anyone outside of that circle overwhelmed me...except my therapist. It was as if my emotions had been exhausted.

I thought I had broken my brain because the dialogue that was usually in my head ceased to exist. One day it was there and the next it was gone. That would have been a good thing, but with it went my short-term memory. I **had** broken my brain.

I was stuck in the present moment, so like my anxiety experiences, I couldn't think right or left, forward or back. I could only concentrate on what was directly in front of me. I could only focus on the task at hand. This was a bit of a nuisance since I was in college completing my degree, hence the medication. It was prescribed to help improve my focus and keep me alert. It did nothing for my memory since my intellect decreased by a letter grade. No matter how long I studied during that time, I wasn't able to earn higher than a B on many exams. It was as if the information just leaked out of my brain. It just wasn't there or it was locked away in a compartment I couldn't access. I actually thought I had burned out neurons in areas of my brain or the neurotransmitters were offline. I wanted to get a brain scan to see exactly what was going on in there. I was fascinated!

During the time after I was diagnosed with depression, I continued to feel and see my physical wellness breaking down. I caught pneumonia. I had shingles. My hair continued to break off and I had bald spots in those areas. I lost my voice at one point and had no idea why. I did not have a cold or sore throat. I had night sweats and started getting migraine headaches before my menstrual period each month. In addition, the premenstrual syndrome that I endured, seemed to last all month. I was usually on edge and felt irritable and cranky most of the time. I began to feel too wired to sleep. I would lie in bed and then get up and have a snack, which was not helpful to my weight release efforts. If I did fall asleep, I would still wake up in the middle of the night to get up and fix a snack.

After I graduated, I couldn't sleep enough. I would sleep for hours in the middle of the day. By that time, I was so exhausted, it was a welcome relief...to parts of my mind and body; however, I was still in "Superwoman mode." It was a challenge to turn it off and it was extremely frustrating for me to not have enough energy to do what I had become accustomed to doing...pushing myself to my limit.

There were mornings I awoke sarcastically thinking, "Great, another day." I felt as if I had nothing to look forward to. I would dread the beginning of the day and couldn't wait to go to bed at night thinking, "I just want to end this day." Some nights I went to bed early, but couldn't fall asleep until hours later. Due to the acid reflux, I had to sleep with an additional pillow under my torso and also sleep on my left side so the acid wouldn't back up into my throat while I slept. This helped some, but I could still feel it at times. After a while, when I lay in bed before sleeping, my stomach would start burning, even if I hadn't had anything spicy. I worried about whether I was developing an ulcer. I needed to do something in order to relax. I read the book, *The Untethered Soul* and practiced an activity in which Michael Singer writes about in the book. I began to pray, meditate, read, and release emotions every evening before bed and began to feel more relaxed as a result.

The more I prayed, meditated, read self-help and inspirational books, and released negative emotions, the more relaxed I began to feel. Once the old familiar dialogue came back (it happened slowly over time), the old negative emotional energy followed. There was more work to do. I needed to listen to the stories that repeated themselves in my mind and examine the emotional baggage that kept me trapped on my roller coaster ride. This is when I realized I had denial dialogue repeating in my mind in every area of my life. It was time to uncover the denials and find out what was really hiding underneath.

I examined my sadness to determine why I felt sad most of the time. I had to become aware of the thoughts attached to that emotion. I wrote about everything I observed and was astounded by what I discovered. I was at the center of my sadness. I initially thought it was the people in my life who were the cause of my suffering, but I was the cause. What I thought and felt about every person I had a relationship with and everything I was involved in caused my sadness. I had a negative thought about almost everything during that time. It couldn't be the people and events that were always wrong, bad, inappropriate, mistaken, imperfect, etc. I was the common denominator. I interpreted everything according to my personal perspective, which was distorted by my interpretation of my experiences. Soon I attached labels and emotions to correlate with my perspective.

I had to change my perspective. Once I realized I needed to change and not everyone and everything around me, I felt the shift that I wrote about earlier in the book. I began to think about what I wanted out of life and how I wanted to feel, to be, and to live. This became my focus. I made the effort to be more empathetic and less judgmental toward people, especially my loved ones. I began to think kind thoughts about myself. I decided to give myself the break that I would give someone else I was in a relationship with. I like myself. I love myself. I thought, why not have a great relationship with myself first? I thought more about the person I wanted to be and less about what I wasn't. I began doing things I enjoyed because I wanted to enjoy life again. The first thing I started doing was dancing again; I had always danced for enjoyment around my house. I downloaded music to my phone and created a dance playlist. Whenever I felt like dancing...I would.

I will admit that I knew I was under some stress, but I was deep in denial about just how much everything I was involved in was affecting me.

I was in denial about all of the excess energy I expended; not having a release for my emotions; not having anyone I could discuss my inner most thoughts with; wanting to solve my own issues without anyone else's input or advice; having almost no down time to just relax; having very few things I found enjoyable, and engaging in them infrequently; denying all of these issues and the feelings connected to each one, was affecting my mind, body, and emotional well-being.

When I felt sad, I was extremely sad. When I was happy, I was still sad. Sadness was my dominant emotion. Anger was the second most dominant and then there was frustration. It was a domino effect beginning with frustration which led to anger, and then ultimately sadness.

The stress from keeping all of these denials hidden took a toll on me, almost driving me over the edge, but not quite. I feel as if I received help in the nick of time. I needed someone to save me from myself. I knew that God was directing my path, however, he required my active participation.

This experience taught me that I couldn't do everything I want to do all at once. It taught me that my mind and emotions are connected to my body and they each influence one another. We tend to ignore, or deny, the chaos that goes on in our minds and pay more attention to the manifestation that shows up in our bodies. Some of us don't even pay attention to the signs we see in or on our bodies (like me). For us, it may take teetering on the edge of sanity to admit that something needs to change.

This experience has also taught me that it is ok to say no. It is ok to say I need some rest. It is ok to feel vulnerable. It is ok to ask for help. It is ok to let other people in (people who care about me).

I have learned that I need a support system of people who care about my well-being and whom I can be of support to. I have heard so often that no man is an island, but some of us think that we are. Often it takes a hard fall to realize we are here to help each other. It is ok to admit when we don't know something. No one on earth knows everything there is to know about everything and everyone. There are those who know a lot about a few things, but not everything. We all need each other to grow. Where else are we going to get the wisdom that comes from living, learning, and adapting to what we encounter during our time here?

Here are a few questions to ponder. They may help you uncover the denials that are reducing your opportunities for expansion in the areas that need it most.

1. Which area of your life feels the most stressful?
2. What are the denials that are active in that area?
3. What are the signs of stress you have noticed in your mind and body or feel as strong emotions?
4. What are your dominant emotions?
5. Which areas of your life are these emotions predominating?
6. What opportunities do you believe you have missed because of your denials?
7. What opportunities are you looking forward to?
8. What are you willing to do today to prepare for new and better opportunities?
9. What are the signs of stress you have noticed in your mind and body or feel as strong emotions?

If you want to delve deeper and uncover the opportunities available to you, I encourage you to complete the questions in our companion guide, *30 Steps For Revealing Denial In Your Life*. and our day book, *The 31-Day Plan for Overcoming Denial*. These books are designed to help you take the necessary steps that can change your life!

Children see the truth behind every denial. I learned at a young age from the people around me that denying the truth is what you do when you don't want other people to know what is really going on behind the curtain. I knew living in denial of things gave me an unnatural, uneasy feeling because it made me feel smaller in some way. It made me want to hide. I was not free to express myself fully. I was taught to deny the truth to the point where I began to distrust myself. "If they are right, then I must be wrong. If they are right, then what I'm feeling must be wrong," is what I thought as a child.

I saw the denial that my parents and other family members lived with and it made them say and do things that were very confusing to me. I witnessed the stories told and the contradictory lives being led. Eventually, I stopped trying to figure out why the adults were not telling the truth about what was really going on in their lives. I stopped acknowledging the truth because no one else did...not in public anyway. I could see both sides of the coin, but I wasn't allowed to speak about either one.

After a while, I wasn't able to speak about much. I stopped talking. I checked out and began to stay in my head, so I would feel safe from the confusion of my life. Have you ever felt that way...like checking out of your life because it is so chockfull of chaos and you are powerless to control it? I know now that was when my denials and control issues began.

I have used denials in every one of the above situations. I think we are all attracted to Denial's charm at some point in our lives and in many areas of our lives. Living in denial can feel natural and if it begins early enough, we may never know we are living in denial. It becomes a way of living...a way of dealing with situations and people...even dealing with ourselves. Denying things that felt uncomfortable to think about, or talk about, kept me from feeling things I didn't want to feel. I did not want to think about things such as what would happen if my dad kept denying the condition of his health and well-being. What would happen if he died because of his declining health? What would happen if my parents physically hurt each other? What would happen if my parents divorced? Keeping those questions out of my conscious awareness kept me from thinking about the answers that increased my fears.

My lovely denials kept me from talking about inconsistencies in the words, actions, and lives of people around me. They kept me moving forward, when I saw little reason to. Living in denial caused me to withdraw a part of myself from the world, but still be able to interact with others, to work and play, although not fully. How could I live fully in one world and also in another I created to keep me—my psyche—intact? Talk about living a double life! That is exactly what it felt like. I was living two lives I created, but one was totally in my head. This allowed me to keep going in spite of the emotional pain I sometimes felt.

I was in sweet denial about many things that I did not want to admit to myself, let alone anyone else. Of course, I had good reasons for maintaining life as it was. The reason denials were so attractive to me was because they satisfied my need to feel as if I had everything under control. It was an allusion, of course. My denials were controlling me; they had me at "Hello" when I discovered I could live in a world of my own creation by using my denials to push away the emotional reality of the present moment, but also deny my responsibility for the condition of my life and the direction it took. I could also deny my responsibility in the condition I was in…my mind, body, and emotions.

I didn't realize I was in denial until I began to see patterns in my life I didn't like. I started to pay more attention to my life when I began to hurt more and enjoy life less. In the meantime, I was mesmerized by my denial's comforting refuge. I wanted to feel good and my denials kept the pain of reality at bay for a while, until I found it necessary to find something to supplement the denials and keep my truth from nagging at me—but it did anyway. I had lived with them for so long that after a time, when my life seemed to be going south and the emotional pain of living in denial began to overwhelm my senses, I supplemented the denials with food to make me feel better. I would relish in all of my favorites to give myself a boost every day and as often during the day as I needed to. Consequently, I began to pack on fat mass that took me years to release.

I know my denials kept me from experiencing life the way I wanted. My denials kept me in a marriage that was no longer alive and thriving; they helped me to overlook my own faults—displeasing attitudes, behaviors, habits, and my inconsistencies. My denials caused me to continue to blame others for my emotional turmoil, circumstances, and situations and kept me feeling disconnected, alienated, rejected, and sad. I could go on, but I won't. You get the picture. For years I thought I felt these things because of other people—how they treated me, how they looked at me, how they spoke to me, if they spoke to me; later I learned (through therapy, mentors, seeking knowledge and wisdom from others, and studying books on psychology, emotion, metaphysics, quantum physics, neuroscience, the Bible, and other book genres), that it wasn't the other people at all who were controlling my destiny, but the thoughts inside my own mind that I didn't want to give a voice to. It was my perceptions (how I interpreted everything) that were causing me to want to deny what I knew to be my truth and accept a beautiful lie instead. I was afraid to acknowledge these thoughts because of my fear of the consequences.

I discovered more about the denials that kept me bound as time passed and began to self-reflect more. I really began burrowing deeper into what was causing me to feel sad and angry after I was diagnosed with depression. Before I was diagnosed, I noticed I kept ending up in the same situations that caused the negative emotions I no longer wanted to feel. I wanted to know why I felt like I was going around in circles instead of moving forward accomplishing my goals and feeling good about my relationships, my life, and myself. I wanted more from life yet I was getting less as time passed.

My Lovely Chamber

For many years I denied my true thoughts and emotions; instead of expressing them, I decided to ignore, suppress, and hide them in my beautiful chamber. I spent more than half of my life suppressing (denying) my emotions and thoughts about situations and people because I believed I was a bad person if I had those thoughts.

Now, because I have been fortunate to have challenges and have learned how to work through them by not only seeking the wisdom of others, but also applying what they have taught me, I know that it is okay to feel emotions—even the ones perceived as negative. I have learned what is most important is managing them wisely. I now realize we are emotional beings, therefore it is all right for me to express my feelings, for example not feeling bad if I do not like someone else's behavior.

I would even feel guilty and ashamed for thinking and feeling negatively toward people who were not kind and loving people. I thought there must be something wrong with me if I was not kind to all people. I believe that was a part of my Christian upbringing though now I know I can love people no matter what they do because we are all deeply connected energetically (spiritually) and at the same time understand their behavior is a reflection of what they have learned and accepted as their perspective of life. I do not have to like, agree with, or condone what they say or how they behave. I don't even have to pretend that their behavior is okay, which is something I used to do. It took time, but now I understand their behavior was a reflection of them and not me. Also, instead of smiling and being indifferent I can confront them about their behavior. It took many years for me to understand that and I spent those years tormenting myself and suppressing (denying) feelings that would have better served me had I allowed myself to express them appropriately.

I subdued my feelings to the point I pushed them to the bottom right corner of my chamber. I didn't feel anything at that point and didn't know how to respond appropriately in many situations. I grew accustomed to hiding my true feelings since I didn't want to give people a reason to dislike me, although I didn't like myself due to my negative feelings, thus people disliking me was inevitable.

Experiencing challenges was not what I was supposed to do considering only unethical people had so-called negative experiences. I thought if I was a virtuous person, I was supposed to live a life of peace and harmony with the birds saluting the sun every morning and chirping their songs of gratefulness. I believed negative experiences should be hidden in my chamber and pretend they did not exist (deny). Additionally, if people knew about my negative experience, they would know I was inferior. Thinking this way caused me to deny many things I disliked about my life. I became a backseat passenger to the circumstances and situations in my life instead of taking the lead and asserting my desire to live well, be well, and have peace of mind by living truthfully.

Journal Entry
October 23, 2013

When I don't eat healthy foods or the correct proportions and accumulate excess fat mass as a result, it's hard on my body. It makes my circulatory system, respiratory system, musculoskeletal system, digestive system, and many others (if not all) work harder to pump blood to these extra places, carry it around, breathe more rapidly to increase the oxygen intake, and thereby oxygen in my blood. When I think about the wear and tear on my body because I am not eating the right foods or correct proportions, it makes me think more about what I'm eating. Putting extra pressure on your systems causes your body to work harder; therefore, it can wear out quicker...aging more rapidly. Thinking about this when I feel hungry helps me to stay on course by eating less and less sugary foods. When I think about wearing out my heart and lungs, and the pressure pressed down on my joints, it makes me think twice, for now.

At this point, I think I'm beginning to finally come back around to wanting to feel and look healthy and fit. I even started rationalizing about teaching classes again. This is a far cry from four years ago when I didn't want to see the inside of a fitness facility let alone really work in one, which is what I went to school to learn how to do better...work with people to reach their exercise goals. What caused this change in my thinking? Is it because I'm reading all of these books? I'm learning considerably about mental health and how the brain works.

I never think about my brain and how there are two separate parts that work to keep me conscious and experiencing life (cognitive brain and emotional brain). These two parts of my brain can also be called the conscious mind and subconscious mind or seat of the intellect and seat of emotions.

The book I'm reading now about healing, anxiety, depression, and stress is so fascinating, I don't want to put it down. It talks about people who may not be emotionally intelligent and how people can suppress their emotional brain so often they find it hard to feel emotion and they can be a little callous when it comes to relating to people because they are unable to read others' emotions. I think that's what happened to me.

I can remember not being able to feel anything except anger. I can remember wondering why I couldn't feel anything. I pressed my emotions down so often and so hard until I could no longer feel them. Examples in the book show situations close to my own where people weren't liked simply because they didn't have...empathy. That's what it is. When you can put yourself in someone else's shoes, you have empathy. That's why I couldn't relate to people; I couldn't understand how they felt as a result of their experiences. Even as a child, I always felt a wall between other children and me...a barrier I could not explain or knew how to penetrate, although I desperately wanted to.

Her Perspective: Poem

Woman Secured
BABY ON THE WAY
I'm clearer now
They're mine, all mine
She ESCAPED once
Anger
BROKEN ARM
I'm clearer now
She's mine, all mine
ASKED TOO MANY QUESTIONS
Rage
Ties that bind Strong
MADE LOVE
I'm clearer now
She's mine, all mine
PROVOCATION
Wrath
BOUQUET OF ROSES

I'm clearer now
She's mine, all mine

Mind your own
She's well, baby's fine
WE'RE HAPPY
I'm clearer now
They're mine, all mine
OUTBURST
Fury
Tumble
Drip on the stair
Her fault, not mine
BABY GONE
SADNESS SWALLOWED
Woman secured
Clearer now.
She's mine, all mine

- Angela Taylor

Read Part II "His Perspective" in my book of Poetry,
Fire of Life: My Awakening Journey

"Courage is resistance to fear, mastery of fear—not absence of fear."
-Mark Twain

Chapter 1

Caught in the Current of Denial

There were many denials that led up to the depression diagnosis and feelings of anxiety that I didn't want to think about. One very important event was not being able to conceive a child. I was in denial about the impact that experience and the following disappointment had on me physically, psychologically, and emotionally. I was in denial about my husband and I growing more distant and the signs my marriage was coming to an end. I denied the fact I had to close my exercise training studio. I denied I was a middle aged, married college student pursuing my Kinesiology degree taking classes with a bunch of nineteen-year olds. I was in denial about the amount of responsibility I already had when I made the choice to become the coordinator to the wellness ministry at my church. This led to an increased level of stress that was already off the charts.

After I graduated, I didn't want to do what I went to school to learn; I lost the drive to teach exercise classes or train people anymore. I was in denial about being burned out and what I wanted my present and future to look and feel like. I denied the life I was living did not fit anymore and about what I wanted to do with the rest of my life or exactly what I wanted that to look like. I was in denial about my role in the condition of my life and the habits I set in place to keep me feeling safe and in control. I was in denial *about* my denials. I was drowning…in my chamber filled with denials.

The stress I felt and the feeling of being overwhelmed and out of control led me to seek help in the form of therapy. I needed an impartial, professional counselor to talk to that would listen and give me knowledgeable, objective, sound, effective advice.

I sought the help of a psychologist who referred me to a psychiatrist for depression medication. I am not one who likes taking any form of medicine even for headaches, so I was not thrilled at the notion of taking it, but I was stressed out and still making an effort to complete my bachelor's degree and we (my therapist and I) both thought medication would help boost my feelings of well-being enough to help me complete school. I thought I would only be taking it for six months until the psychiatrist told me it took at least a few months for it to get into my system and begin to work. After my first prescription, the dosages changed throughout the years. Now, at the time I am writing this book, I am taking the minimum maintenance dose and look forward to the day when I no longer need it.

I decided after a while in therapy with my psychologist to discontinue sessions with her and to continue sessions with the psychiatrist. I felt like the effectiveness of our sessions was waning and I had resolved as much as I could under her direction. I was still taking medication and needed to continue discussing my progress with the psychiatrist, which worked out well.

I was able to continue progressing, which, to me, was "getting better." I had to adopt some new habits that would assist me in feeling better yet I couldn't get a handle on the one that should have been the easiest for me—establishing an exercise routine.

I was too exhausted at the time and had to wait until I felt like I had the energy to exercise. This took some time and since I was an exercise instructor and personal trainer, I beat myself up every day for not feeling up to it. This, of course, added to my stress, which was counter-productive to my recovery, but I wanted to feel better so badly that I would exercise whenever I felt a little energy until it became more consistent.

My humble advice to you is if you have seen a therapist and didn't see any improvement in your state of mind, or if you are still seeing a therapist and don't seem to be making any progress that will improve your life, consider seeking another therapist until you find the one who is the right fit for you. Just because one didn't work, doesn't mean therapy doesn't work. Each therapist has his or her own personal and professional experience he or she brings to the sessions and this unique quality appeals to different types of people. One size does not fit all when it comes to therapy or therapists. Would you continue seeing your medical doctor if you weren't feeling any better under his or her care? Well, unfortunately some people do, but not you, because you want results. You *want* to get better. If something feels off, make inquiries into other therapists. It may mean you haven't located the right one for you, yet, or maybe you need another form of therapy. Explore your options. Group therapy works for some (it seemed to keep me in the same state of mind. I needed more one-on-one interaction so I could ask questions and apply what I had learned immediately. Group therapy may help if you need a support group that makes you feel as if you have people who understand what you are going through. Getting things off of my chest was what I needed most). You could also seek information from self-help books and experiment with natural forms of therapy. Find something that works for *you*!

It doesn't matter what did or did not work for someone else; sometimes we spend too much time thinking about what others have said or done, but it is important to remember that we are all individuals and what works for someone else may not work for you and vice versa. You have to give yourself some time to begin to feel better. I felt better almost immediately by talking about what I was feeling and what I had been through. I needed a person that would be impartial and have the knowledge I needed to help maintain or increase the momentum of my recovery. I looked forward to sharing more at every session with my psychologist and anticipated what she had to say.

Remember to never give up on yourself. If you desperately want to change, you will do what you have to in order to improve your life. If you don't do it for yourself, who will?

Denial will keep us hostage until the day we die; the majority of us already have our hands bound by Denial. Those of us living the bulk of our lives in denial, ignore all the signs and signals shouting out to us that something needs to change or something isn't right. We may be in a physically, mentally, or emotionally abusive relationship; disregarding the truth that our job or career is inappropriate for us; not eating properly, getting enough rest, or exercising, et cetera, et cetera. These denials that we allow to bind us will continue to do so unless we take a stand and break the bondages.

However, we ignore our truths, even when we realize we are experiencing the same types of relationships, ending up in the same situations, burdened with the same circumstances that we always have. Yet, some of us refuse to make any changes leading to a more rewarding and lucrative life in our job or career, supportive and harmonious friendships, loving relationships, more money, peace of mind, happiness, joy...I could go on and on.

We can habitually live our lives in circles—hiding and denying. For instance, when we think we have found someone new or tried a new way of doing things, we circle around to our familiar habits and end up back where we started. Why? Simply because we haven't self-reflected or examined the responsibility we have in choosing the condition of our lives.

Many of us are unaware that our circumstances can change and we are responsible for changing them. We are living our lives according to what our previous experiences have taught us, continuing the same old thought patterns controlling the outcome of our lives. The pattern will only stop when we decide something needs to change; however, our denials keep us on the merry-go-round because they have improved in their positions by years of on-the-job training and maintaining the status quo. A further chapter in the book will look inside your brain explaining how these patterns are formed and how much of a challenge it can be to change them, but not an impossible feat.

My denials led me to make poor choices since I was ignoring the still small voice in my head even when I knew it was right. How did I know it was right? The answer benefitted all concerned, came with a sense of peace, and decreased the anxiety I felt surrounding that particular challenge. Yet, after the calm, I would feel a storm of anxiety. My fears would resurface, permitting the denials to push forward out of the hole in which they were hiding. Let me clarify, my truth came in peace, but when I started thinking about what it would take to live my truth, my attention immediately went to the challenges I would have to overcome and the ramifications of the actions I would need to take after making the choice to live authentically. I knew there would be people in my life who would not appreciate me changing their lives so drastically and of course I wanted to be considerate and not selfish, so I gave in and kept the denials in place.

The obstacles I thought were blocking my way stopped me from formulating any lasting changes to my life; that's where the doubt and anxiety came from.

My Denials

I consciously refused to acknowledge my issues because thinking about them felt uncomfortable. Acknowledging the truth could have led to making some tough decisions, which would have been uncomfortable. I justified it by thinking, "It's better not to rock the boat after all; it isn't that bad."

I denied:

- Responsibility for my own life.
- My unhappiness.
- The relationship I was in wasn't working.
- My emotions.
- My intuition.
- Responsibility for my situations and circumstances.
- My stress.
- My lack of control of my life.
- Eating to feel better.
- Gaining a lot of weight.
- Wanting a different life.

I knew inside that certain relationships and situations weren't right for me, but I pushed the feelings aside and continued with the status quo because:

- I wanted to prove marriages didn't have to end.
- I was afraid of change.
- I wasn't prepared to leave.
- I was afraid of what others would think.
- I would have to make some drastic changes.
- I wasn't ready to change.
- I believed in someone else's opinions over my own.
- I didn't connect my past experiences with my current experience, nor the depression diagnosis.
- I continued to blame everyone around me for my pain.
- I learned to push down my true thoughts and emotions.
- I learned to ignore my intuition.
- I did not want anyone to know how lonely I was.
- I did not want anyone to know I felt unloved and unlovable.
- I was extremely self-conscious.
- I did not want anyone to know I felt inadequate.
- I did not want to admit I felt sad and neglected.
- I did not want to admit that my life was not as perfect as I pretended it to be.

Journal Entry

January 2014

While reading and re-typing my journal stories into my computer, I realized how much I was in denial about my life, what I was actually going through, and why. I wrote about support I had, but didn't see how inconsistent it was. I wrote about needing to lose weight almost in every entry. Although I have released some of the weight I gained as a result of the hormones, I'm still struggling with the same ten to fifteen pounds of weight. I realize I am no longer in my twenties and don't need as many calories to keep me energized and healthy, but I'm still eating the same amount of food I began eating a few years before I left my previous position at the insurance company. I began picking up weight because I hated the monotony of sitting at a desk all day. I wanted to leave my job, but knew my household would not be able to survive, especially since I didn't have another job replacement. It has been a pattern with me to endure something almost unbearable until I could not endure it anymore, feeling as if I would lose my mind if I didn't get out at that moment. Well, even though I found a career worth pursuing and enjoyed before I left, it didn't pay as much compared to my salary at the insurance company.

In addition, I was not happy in my marriage; I was often met with condescension and hostility. I remember my husband and I having lunch toward the end of my career at the insurance company and after lunch I would always wonder to myself why I returned to the office feeling so dreadful. I usually went back to work feeling just as or more depressed than I was before I left, but in my journals I always wrote about the understanding and support I received. I wondered what in the world I was I talking about and then I realized I wrote that because I received assistance with house chores or other responsibilities, but I felt like understanding, respect, and emotional support were lacking. I believe that's when I began to feel abandoned emotionally. I no longer felt like I could discuss issues important to me so, I stopped trying. I no longer felt the connection we once had.

I don't know when we stopped talking to one another and being friends; I can't put my finger on any one thing that happened. It was probably an accumulation of things throughout the years. Neither one of us liked confrontations; for me it stemmed from my childhood and constantly feeling self-conscious. As a result, we just let things fester and handled them in a passive-aggressive way.

My thoughts focused on not angering or disturbing anyone in any way for fear they may try to hurt me in some way. I tried to become invisible as a child; I kept quiet and became introverted and eventually I began to feel invisible, yet I wanted to be noticed, acknowledged, and understood. As far back as I can remember, I felt like I had more inside of me than I was expressing or allowed to express. Thus, I stopped expressing myself and suppressed my inquisitive nature. I couldn't seem to find the words to express my thoughts; I had many questions, but rarely asked any and retreated into my world, making my own answers. My teachers in grade school and high school would report to my mom that they would forget I was there because I never said anything in class and they didn't know how smart I was until they received my homework. One of my teachers even gave me a bad grade on a homework paper that I thought was pretty good and instead of saying anything about it to him, I just thought, "Oh well, I guess it wasn't as good as I thought." After he handed all of the homework papers back, he called me up to his desk and told me he purposely gave me a poor grade just to see if I would say anything about it, but I didn't. I remember he gave me a D, but I actually earned an E for excellent. I automatically thought I was mistaken, even though I felt like I had done a good job. Why?

I'm not a psychologist or psychiatrist, but I don't suspect I started out as a shy, introverted child, but rather metamorphosed into one due to the circumstances I lived under. Why did I worry about myself so much? Why did I compare myself to other people so often? Why wasn't I comfortable sharing my thoughts with others? Why did I automatically think I was wrong and someone else was right even though that clearly wasn't the case? When did I stop being an inquisitive kid or showing up and making my presence known? When did I begin to distrust my own intuition? When did I stop believing in myself? I remember feeling like I was a bad person if I asked questions or spoke up. I also remember thinking I was a bad person if I was honest about how I felt about people who I didn't like or who treated me poorly. I thought that I was a bad person if I even thought bad things about anyone, so I tried to be a good little girl and <u>act</u> nice. That's what I did, no matter what anyone said or did to me; I would excuse their behavior and believe they did it because of something I did or said or simply because they didn't like me. I would have never deemed a person just as a mean person, even when I knew it in my heart. It was always my fault, so I vanished, disappeared as to not cause other people to be cruel to me or cause me pain.

This makes me mourn for my self-esteem and self-worth. As I'm typing these words, which are just pouring from my soul, my eyes are welling up with tears because I feel heartbroken for this little girl...me, in an adult body.

I knew I was just as intelligent, but for some reason I thought of myself as deficient. I knew it wasn't true, yet I believed it anyway, hoping no one else would find out. Who told me as a child that I wasn't smart? Where did that label come from? How many other children are labeled dumb, yet it is not true, but someone else said it or implied it in some way? I compared myself to other children and felt inadequate because I thought I didn't have something they had, that made them better in some way. I didn't have the answers, but I had a lot of questions. I'm not afraid to ask them now, but will I ever get answers and does it really matter anyway at this point?

I've felt these things, but I've never written them down or voiced them to anyone until now. I don't even know why this is coming out at this time, but I'm glad that it is. There's healing in releasing thoughts and emotions that have been locked up inside the subconscious for so long. I'm going to stop typing now to have a good cry.

Denial, First in the Stages of Grief Model

Denial is listed as the first stage of grief, which is an emotional reaction to the experience of a loss such as when a loved one dies, the loss of a job, divorce, disease, drug addiction, incarceration, etc. It is one of the five stages of grief model introduced by Dr. Elisabeth Kubler-Ross in her book inspired by her work with the terminally ill written in 1969 entitled, *On Death and Dying.* She however expanded the model to include any type of loss. She states in her book the order of the stages is not set in stone, and may occur together or overlap, if they occur at all. So, if you are in the denial stage and next on the list is anger, you may or may not experience it or you may have anger as a side dish with denial as the main course.

One of her quotes listed on her foundation's website is, "When you learn your lessons, the pain goes away." It can take a mountain to fall on us before we get it, but when we decide to acknowledge the truth, we can begin to move through denial toward recovery.

Beneficial Denials

In the article "Denial: When it helps, When it hurts," written by the Mayo Clinic Staff and posted on mayoclinic.org., it states, "Denial, when used as a coping mechanism, can help us adjust to the situation or keep us from dealing with a situation." According to the article, short-term denial can be a good thing because it gives you time to adjust to a situation that may be stressful or painful to think about. It is a way for your mind to absorb distressing information without breaking down under the pressure. For example, if someone you love dies unexpectedly, you may need some time to process the information and begin to assess what challenges may exist ahead. In this way, denial can be an initial response to a situation that helps you come to terms with what has happened, subsequently approaching the subject more logically in order to decide what needs to be done before taking action. However, being in denial for too long can be harmful because it prevents you from dealing with the situation by not taking action to resolve it. An example of unhealthy denial listed by the Mayo Clinic is the parents of a young daughter with a drug addiction continuing to provide her "clothing" money. In this example, the denial keeps their daughter from getting the help she needs, which can cause her condition and actions to spiral out of control, potentially causing detrimental long-term results.

Denial can be helpful when it is temporary, for it allows us the chance to step back and regroup before taking action. However, denying an issue is also a common rationale for us to avoid asking for help or seeking needed treatment. If it continues, it can keep us from planning an appropriate resolution and moving ahead with our lives.

Buried Denials

According to an article listed on the Psych Central website, "Roots of denial can be buried deep within a person's sense of who they are and how they were brought up to view themselves, and the world around them." It's nothing nowadays for a man to ask his doctor for Viagra to help him perform better sexually, but the same man may go into denial and turn to alcohol or drugs to deal with his depression. A woman will schedule her annual mammogram for early detection of breast cancer, but will deny that her excessive eating is possibly an emotional issue. It may take hitting rock bottom, getting to the end of our rope, having our back up against the wall, or feeling completely hopeless and miserable with the only way out is through the choice to live or die before we decide something needs to change. The article also states it is common to give an excuse such as, "I just haven't been getting enough sleep," when the truth is you are depressed and have used the same excuse for months.

Brain Plasticity and Denial

Although the more scientists study the brain, the more questions they have; scientific studies are ongoing and have resulted in some insight into the brain's inner workings. Recent studies show that the structure of our brain actually changes as we learn, whether from books or interacting with our environment (experience), including emotional interactions. In addition, according to the book, *Neuroplasticity*, parts of the brain can compensate for areas damaged due to injury or disease and restructure the brain creating additional neural networks in order to restore a function or functions that have been lost. Also, some areas of the brain have the ability to take over the functions of another damaged area.

We are born with billions of brain cells, which when stimulated by words, phrases, actions, or emotions, causes our brain to change, forming new neural pathways. "If the stimulus is repeated often enough, it can help solidify recall of this new information. This is a primary mechanism in which children learn." As we continue to gain knowledge, some neural connections that aren't stimulated by our environment get discarded, while those that are stimulated, or inherited through genetic programs, strengthen as they grow and mature." (Brain Plasticity, 167)

The ability of the brain to respond to input and change its physical structure, generate, and re-route neurons and their networks to restore function lost by other areas of the brain is called "plasticity." It was once thought the brain was not capable of changing once we hit a certain age, but recent studies show the brain continues to develop after birth and changes throughout our lives. As we expand our knowledge by activities such as learning how to play a musical instrument, learning to speak a new language, or exposing ourselves to different environments or social situations with a variety of groups of people, for instance, our brain responds to this input and restructures its neural networks to accommodate additional neurons and connections that support the new information.

When we begin to analyze our thoughts, we can discover patterns of thinking. The patterns created by our thinking are formed by our unconscious habitual thoughts that go unmonitored and uncensored. This pattern of habitual thinking is not a conscious process, however, we can become aware of it just by paying attention to our thoughts. This pattern of thinking physically restructures the brain while we are thinking. The repeated stimulation of neurons created by our thoughts form network connections that become stronger and react quicker over time including the emotions we feel. In essence, the way we think becomes habitual, which is a challenge to break; however, it can be changed over time and with conscious effort and determination.

How does this tie in with denial? When we live in denial for a long period of time, our denial stories may become the fairytales, bedtime stories, or daytime dramas we repeat to everyone around us (including our children) and ourselves for years and even decades. Our stories are reinforced by neural connections in the brain that were created by repeating these stories over and over and feeling the emotions that coincide with them. This can make the denial stories a challenge to change, though, not impossible.

We are born with the basic structures, but it is important for our environment to provide the correct stimulation during certain intervals of brain development for children called critical intervals and sensitive intervals. In the book, *The Everything Guide to the Human Brain,* the author, Rudolph C. Hatfield, PhD, writes, "A very important feature of development is experience. Instructive experiences will direct the development, whereas permissive experiences are required for a genetic program to be activated." He explains that experiences must occur within a particular time period (critical) to be effective, and some experiences are more effective during a particular time period, but may still have weakened effects outside of that period (sensitive).

The book also cites a case to help his readers understand the importance of these intervals. The case involves Genie, a little girl who was severely neglected by both parents and physically abused by her father.

Genie was tied to a toilet in a small dark room most days from the time she was twenty months old. Her mother was blind and only spent a few minutes a day with her to feed her. In the evening, she was put in a straitjacket and placed into a covered crib. Her father rarely spoke to her and if she made any noise at all he would beat her. Genie received very limited stimulation. When she was thirteen-years old, she weighed only sixty-two pounds and was less than four-and-a-half-feet tall when she was found. She was not able to stand alone or chew solid food, and had no bowel or bladder control. Due to the severe deprivation, she had major challenges learning language and she never learned typical forms of behavior like personal hygiene or how to control her anger.

Although Genie's case is extreme, the point I am making is that our environment plays a large role in our motor skill development, physical development, activities of daily living (including personal hygiene), language and speech development and structure and promotes emotional development important for social skills and forming lasting relationships.

Our mental, physical, and emotional development, behaviors, and ultimately the way we live our lives, depends on the nurturing we received from the people in our environment(s) as children.

If the people closest to us when we were children lived in denial, how does that affect us?

- What did you learn from your childhood environment?
- What denial stories did you grow up listening to?
- What denial stories are you still telling?
- What are the situations, circumstances, conversations, events, activities, attitudes, or behaviors in your past that you have chosen not to face because of the pain involved?

If you are not ready to face the denials, it is okay; it may take some time before you are ready. If you want to examine your life and past a little deeper, but need help, seeking a professional therapist who can assist you in making different choices could lead to a better life.

I will often say throughout this book that if one therapist did not help you, that does not mean there is not one who can. It is important to follow the advice we receive, for if you don't try it, you won't know whether or not it works. Keep searching until you find the right professional psychologist, psychiatrist, or other mental health professional that can help you. Remember, group therapy is also an option. I want to add, be sure that whichever path you take toward a better understanding you think will potentially lead to your healing, is doing exactly that. If you are working with your issues and following the guidance of your therapist though you are not feeling any better after acknowledging your issues, examining your life and making the necessary changes (reducing stress, getting enough sleep, exercising, etc.), look into other alternatives like medication (pharmaceutical or natural) and ask about other forms of therapy. Keep the momentum moving forward and find the best method of healing/recovery/restoration for you.

Coming out of denial and acknowledging our truth can be the first step to freedom, but there may be many more steps before you get to where you want to be. Be patient with yourself. One step at a time, inch by inch... be consistent and persistent. Always know that what you want may be on the next landing, down the street, or around the corner, keep moving until you see the future you want come into view.

Relationships in Denial

In an article written by Benedict Carey for The New York Times website on November 20, 2007 entitled, "Denial Makes the World Go Round," Carey states that recent studies […] suggest the ability to look the other way (deny), while potentially destructive, is also critically important to forming and nourishing close relationships. We sometimes disregard, rationalize, minimize, or reframe infractions with friends, and especially with a spouse or partner, in order to continue with the relationship and stay in our happy place. The challenge arises when the denials keep us from being healthy, moving on, getting the help we need, changing unwanted behavior, or helping someone whose denials are potentially harmful or dangerous to them, to others, and/or to us.

Socially Acceptable Denials

The New York Times article also mentions reframing and states that it involves denial and a little touch-up work, for example, seeing jealousy as passion. What adult hasn't done that a time or two? Within the same article there is a statement given by Eviatar Zerubavel, a sociologist at Rutgers University, explaining how decorum, tact, politeness, and subjects considered to be taboo, limit what can be said in our social groups and reduces the space in which silence can be broken. Basically, the longer we stay silent, the easier it becomes to continue denying and the more difficult it is to keep it hidden.

Denying the Appearance

A denial can be used as a method to change a negative pattern of thought. We can do this by using a statement rejecting the appearance of an unfortunate situation and following it with a statement proclaiming what we want to experience instead, Denials and Affirmations.

I used denials to ignore the appearance of what I didn't want and affirmations to keep in mind what I did want, but without applying it to my every day, moment-to-moment life. I was brought up as a Christian under the non-denominational heading of "New Thought" or "Practical Christianity," which makes the individual an active participant (working as an individual expression of all that God is) in our lives instead of being passive and waiting on God to do something to help us. "New Thought" Christians know that with the power of God working in and through us as us, we can do, be, accomplish, or establish what we <u>know</u> we can. We know that God has given us all of the tools here on earth for us to live the lives we want. Others have adopted this way of thinking and behaving, but may not call themselves "New Thought" Christians, Christians, or religious believers at all. A label is just a label. What matters are the results we all receive from what we know and practice. Our lives reflect what we believe.

As a "New Thought" Christian, I was confused for many years about the practice of denials and affirmations. I understood the practice was to denounce the appearance of what we may have seen as a negative circumstance and affirm the Truth (all of the good that God is), but I also thought that meant we were supposed to ignore things that needed to be recognized and acted on, which to me was lying and hiding. As a "New Thought" Christian, I had not applied the principles that were a cornerstone to our teaching. What we know can only be activated when we practice it. I also had to work with, practice, and use what I professed and knew to be true.

As a "New Thought" Christian, putting principle into practice can be the most challenging thing to do. On the surface, it seems as if we are being told to ignore the appearance and imagine what we really want happening in our lives when that is only the superficial layer. We are placing an order with the creator, praying, and calling forth our good into physical existence from the quantum realm. It is important that we be specific and authentically feel how it will be to have what we choose from our menu of choices. We are also to do the work necessary to bring about what we really want to experience in our lives and let go of the things that are not working. For instance, if I want to become a professional medical doctor, I need to go to school and not quit until I have received that doctoral certificate in my hand. If I want to become a doctor and never go to college or apply to medical school, I will only be able to practice being a doctor in my imagination or risk going to prison for impersonating one. It would be unwise to practice something I am not equipped to practice, subjecting my life and the lives of my family to ridicule, rejection, and lost opportunities in addition to the loss of my freedom. It is necessary for me to decide I am going to do the work and receive all of the benefits that come with becoming a doctor the correct and lawful way. This applies to everything we want to experience in life.

Using denials in order to reprogram and refocus our mind can benefit us as long as we are aware that effects have causes. The cause may be genetic, environmental, or psychological. When we continue to deny something we don't want to acknowledge, and at the same time refuse to examine the underlying cause, this can lead to a life of denial and our challenges, whether physical, mental, emotional, or environmental, may not change and could possibly worsen.

The cause creating the effect we are experiencing has to change or be eliminated before we see the changes we affirm. For instance, if we are unable to pay our car note, mortgage, or rent on time because of overspending, any excess money we may receive, (inheritance, raise, or lottery win) will be spent unwisely, unless we learn how to manage our money more effectively. In this case, if we continue denying the appearance of not having enough, but do nothing to change the behavior that is causing it, we will more than likely continue to experience the same results in our lives no matter how much money we receive. Thus, if I am helping a loved one on a regular basis to pay his or her bills and I can't understand where the money is going, I need to ask questions. It is unwise to continue to throw money at an issue with a cause that may have nothing to do with the amount of money the person is making or receiving. Is the person mismanaging the money? Does he or she have a habit that needs to be addressed? Is the money being given away or invested in something ill advised? It would be wise for me to ask questions before I give money or continue to give money to what appears to be a money issue, though it may not be. On the other hand, if I know I need assistance with managing my finances, it would be important for me to come out of denial so that I could be financially free and experience the peace that comes with acknowledging my truth and getting the assistance needed in order to become financially independent. Here is another example: if I am experiencing pain in my body or have been diagnosed with a physical or mental challenge, I may decide to ignore the facts. If I do not examine possible causes for the signs and symptoms I feel and research health, wellness, and healing treatments that will restore me to optimal health, I may continue experiencing discomfort and disease. I would be denying the effects, ignoring the causes, and thereby delaying my healing and path to recovery and vitality. Yes, I believe in healing. I know that when we really believe (know) something is possible, anything can happen. That is what the placebo effect shows. We can change our experiences using the power of our belief, but it is unwise to bury our heads in the sand hoping, praying, and wishing for change when the answer is right under our noses, yet we refuse to uncover it and act on it.

Denial Briefs

These are examples of short denial stories. The intention is for you to understand what denial looks like in a variety of situations.

- While showering this morning, I discovered the lump I have in my armpit has grown larger. I have been putting off going to the doctor because I'm afraid of what it might be. I'll stop using my deodorant or switch to another brand and see whether it goes down after a month or so. If it doesn't, then I'll go to the doctor.

- I have this pain in my upper abdomen on the right side and I don't know what it is. It doesn't feel like indigestion; I know what that feels like. This is something else. I've been taking these herbs my friend Julie has and swears by, but they don't seem to be working. I don't know what else to do, I don't like doctors. I don't want to go see one since all they do is write prescriptions. I don't want to take any medication. Maybe I just haven't found the right herb yet. I'll find out what else Julie has and see if that will help.

- I have been having pain when I urinate, but I don't want anyone to know. I've had it ever since I had sex with that girl I met at my friend's birthday party. I think she may have given me something, but I don't know. It's been almost two weeks now and it hasn't gone away. I'll give it another week and if it doesn't stop, I'll call my doctor.

- I won't answer the phone today. I didn't pay the credit card bill this month. I needed the money to buy new shoes for that celebration at the church last Sunday. They'll get their money when I get paid in two weeks, so better yet, I won't answer the phone until I get paid.

- "Why are you calling him again? I thought the two of you broke up last week." "He just said he needed some space, so I didn't call him for two days. I think that's enough space. I usually call him every day."

- I know I am late for work every day and I come in late from lunch, but I do my work. It's not my fault my coworkers are idiots. I don't know why some of them were even hired. They're such losers. So I have had an argument with a few of them; they need to learn how to do their jobs correctly and I wouldn't have to tell them how to do it! I'm a valuable member of the team. They wouldn't fire me—I'm an asset. If they fired me, they wouldn't function! I have over twenty years of experience.

- I can't stand those people. Why can't they just get it like the rest of us? Why do they have to make everything so hard? It's their fault they can't get ahead. Look at *me*—I came from nothing. I worked hard and now I own half the town and most of the next one. If I can do it, anyone can. They need to get their act together and stop being so lazy.

A Denial Story Reenactment

"Passing the Buck"

Shut the ---- up. I'll give you something to cry about. Get your little — in the car like I told you. What the ---- are you crying about? I don't care who hit you. You probably deserved it. You are always hitting somebody else and now you want to cry because somebody hit you back. I told you about that. Now, get in the ------ car before I hit you myself.

Later in school

Teacher: Sit down Jeff.

Jeff: I don't have to sit because you say so. ---- you!

Teacher: What did you say? I'm going to call your mom!

After School

Teacher: Yes, Mrs. Decker?

Parent: Yes, who is this?

Teacher: This is Mrs. Kelly from Canfield Elementary. I'm Jeffery's teacher. Do you have a moment to talk?

Parent: What is it? What has he done now?

Teacher: I just wanted to talk to you about his behavior and language in class.

Parent: What about it?

Teacher: He's been talking while I'm teaching, fighting with the other students, and now he has resorted to cursing at me. I've never experienced this kind of behavior from him before. Is there something going on at home that could be causing it?

Parent: Are you trying to blame me for his behavior? Isn't that what you're there for, to teach him? So, teach him. Everything is fine at home. I don't have any problems with him. Maybe you just need to learn how to handle him. Don't try to blame me for your-------failures. Is there anything else?

Teacher: Well, I…

Parent: Good. Bye!

*****

I don't like that side of the family anyway. Why do they want to come over here, to be nosy? That's probably it, because they've never wanted to come here before. I told Jessica, Aunt Kate, and Cousin Lucile I couldn't stand them since they are always in somebody else's business. So, I let Mike discipline Jeff. He's the man of the house. His real father isn't around. Mike is the only one he'll listen to. So he tells Jeff he's just like his father—a loser. He is a loser and Jeff will be just like him. He has his ways. My family just gets on my nerves; going to try to tell me how to run my business when she's looking like a cow. Jessica needs to stop eating. I'm sure Gary doesn't want a fat girlfriend. She had better watch out because I have my eyes on him. When she slips up, I'll be right there. I don't care if she is my cousin. She isn't my friend, no love lost between us. What Mike don't know won't hurt him. Gary is fine, and he's nothing like Mike.

Someone else: "I heard he's verbally abusive to her kids just like Mike is to yours and he hits her. Why would you want to go from bad to worse?"

Please, that ain't nothing I haven't been through and can't handle. Mike tries to get physical, but I give it right back to him. I can handle myself.

Deny's Dream

Suspended Animation

Meet Deny, Part 1: Poem

Deny is the grand dame of the denial agency.
She has been around since the beginning of man
And has grown more sophisticated
And complicated with each millennium.
No nonsense and all nonsense;
Clever, skillful, and intelligent,
She is the master at her craft.
The guru, the oracle of secrets,
He has many apprentices, agents that do his bidding.
Covert and adaptable, they are loyal to their "Elizabeth,"
Queen and commander, director of operations.

Leading from his throne,
He can conquer and claim spaces devoid of truth
For her kingdom.
The director of our madness,
Her discourse overtakes our souls.
She can make us feel like gods and goddesses
And then take us to depths only told
By those of us who have escaped his influence,
Some cracked, some broken,
But all heroes to those of us
Who are still controlled by her narrative.
The awareness, determination, and diligence
Of these exceptional individuals
Have lived to experience her intent,
Played out in perfect synchronicity.
She can be the opinion we cling to in the morning
And the utterance we despise at night.

He works toward her goal, ceaselessly
To permeate our thoughts
With her interpretation of our encounters.
She conceals, suppresses, and rejects our truth;
She wants to help us any way she can
And believes she knows what is best for us.
He is so efficient at his job that she
Makes us believe her vision is real.
The emotions we feel from the stories
He tells add a layer of credibility that wins us over
And lowers our guard.
She is the specter orator,
Apparition physician with an invisible stethoscope

A shadow friend, a wraith wearing a fabricated cloak
And we are undeniably her captive audience.
                                        - Angela Taylor

> "He who conquers others is strong; he who conquers himself is mighty."
>
> **- Lao Tzu**

Chapter 2

Beauty and Vanity of My Denial

The Beauty and Vanity of a Denial

I look at my reflection in the full-length mirror. I am wearing a soft blue Mulberry silk cocktail dress that accentuates my curves, which are lightly scented with Clive Christian No. 1. The mirror and frame were especially designed for me; the frame carved from extravagant African Blackheart and Purpleheart wood, contoured in the form of doves displayed with wings spread, as if gliding on air. The wings have streaks of gold lining the tops of the feathers, simulating the highlights of the sun while in flight.

At my request, the mirror was placed in the right corner of the front entryway with two crystal chandeliered spotlights suspended above. I want to get a glance of myself as I strut, with my head tilted upward and shoulders pulled back, the posture of a queen. The professional interior designer I hired three years ago created this area of my entrance. I admire the image I see staring back at me and exclaim, "I am a Queen! Makeda (Queen of Sheba) has nothing on me!" I blow myself a kiss and prance out of the door into my Rolls-Royce Phantom...door held open by my chauffeur. As I sit and look back at my dwelling, I notice broken bricks on the cracked pavement and the garden of overgrown weeds in my yard and say, "Where did those come from?" I look up and realize the bricks are from my chimney. I knew that the mortar had worn partially away, but the bricks I thought were still secure.

My chauffeur, in his new off-white uniform I chose to coordinate with the Rolls, walks around the car, gets in and puts the car in drive. As he begins to drive away, I yell, "Stop!" He presses the brake and asks, "Is everything ok, madam?" "No, it is not!" I yell at him. "This place...this place is hideous. Where am I? Am I in a nightmare? What is going on? This is not my house! This is a shack and it looks uninhabited. Why is this monstrosity leaning to one side? Where is the second floor and balcony overlooking the fountain from Italy I had created of my likeness? Someone has stolen my fountain! Why is the door cracked down the middle? It has no knob or lock. What is that brown fluid dripping from it? The paint on this thing is dark gray and is chipped and scattered all over the ground! My house is not gray; it is white with a pale yellow trim along the top and electric yellow painted around the...where are the windows? Why is there dirt everywhere? What has happened to my freshly mown green lawn? I watched my gardener mow it while I sat upstairs drinking coffee on the balcony of my bedroom, just this morning. Where are my gardens, pond, and evergreens? What is going on?"

I heard a noise and turned to see where it came from. I opened my eyes to see a room filled with people sitting on mats staring at me while my best friend Mona stood over me. I was in the front of the Yoga room. The last thing I remembered was that I had closed my eyes for meditation at the end of the Yoga practice. *How did I get up here?* I thought to myself. Embarrassed, I grabbed my towel and bottle of water and quickly rolled up my mat while looking down at the floor. I didn't want to see their faces. By their expressions when I opened my eyes, I knew I had ruined meditation for them. I could hear them whispering as I prepared to leave the room. Walking out of the door I heard someone say, "Maybe she's schizophrenic and forgot to take her meds this morning."

I hurried out of the Yoga room and straight to the locker room with Mona closely trailing behind. "Ann, what happened in there?" my friend Mona asked.

I sat on the bench in front of my locker, put the towel up to my face and began to cry. "I've never been so embarrassed in my life. I don't know what happened. What did I do? Why were they staring at me? Why was I in front of the room?"

"You stood up on your mat as if looking at yourself in a mirror and said something about the Queen of Sheba. I almost laughed out loud when I heard you say that. I knew that African history documentary we watched would have an impact, but I never thought everyone in our Yoga class would hear about it," Mona snickered.

"I can't believe I did that. I will never be able to come here again."

"That isn't the half of it," Mona said. "You walked up to the front of the room, sat on the floor facing the door, turned, and looked around as if you were looking at something very large, and then told someone to stop. I wasn't sure what to do. I thought maybe you were having a nervous breakdown or were sleepwalking. I heard it could be dangerous to wake people up who sleep walk. So, I slowly made my way to where you were, trying to figure out what to do, and you began asking someone questions about a shack with a cracked door and no windows. Oh yeah, you also wanted to know what happened to the balcony and fountain of yourself that you brought back from Italy. By that time, I started calling your name and telling you to wake up. You finally snapped out of it when I clapped my hands."

"Oh, no, no, no! I don't understand Mona. Why did that happen? Am I losing my mind? I know I have been going through a lot lately, but this... this is crazy!"

"It will be ok, Ann. I know what you have been going through and it is just taking a toll on your mind.

You have been trying not to let it get to you, but it is too much to handle. The chaos you are living in has to show up somehow, no matter how hard you try to hide it. You cannot continue denying the situation you are in anymore. It does not matter what other people will say or do. You need to get help, so that you can be free." "But, Mona I don't want anyone to know what I have been living with."

"Look Ann. You have put up a good front. No one would ever know you have been living the way you have, but think about what has just happened. Everyone in that room knows something is going on underneath the calm cool mask you hide behind. Don't you see that something has to be done, now? You know I will always have your back. You have to face this, so that this never happens again or God forbid, something worse. So, what do you want to do and how can I help?"

The Beauty of Denial

At some point, if nothing changes, we may begin to see and feel the signs and symptoms which can lead to embarrassing situations like Ann and Mona's experience in Yoga class.

The longer we attempt to maintain our silence, the sooner the denials begin to cause us to behave in ways that may be undetected by us and others at first, but eventually can be seen quite clearly.

The world we create (by denying) may not look exactly the way we want it to, but it feels better than we imagine the alternative would feel. In this world, we can push away anything too painful to look at and feel. The depth of emotion we anticipate will overwhelm our senses, contaminate our thoughts, and cause changes we may not be ready to deal with. Living within the beauty of denial allows us to continue to work; interact with and maintain our familial relationships, friendships, and love relationships; attend church functions; attend social events; pay bills; shop; take care of our children; manage groups of people; maintain an efficient and organized household; pursue entrepreneurial endeavors; pray and meditate; preach; teach; go to school; perform our civic duties; volunteer; counsel; mentor; and otherwise handle the myriad of responsibilities we adopt.

Living in denial can also cause us to continue to overindulge in things that help us bury our denials and feel good for a few moments. This life can extend into days, weeks, months, years, and decades. We may find ourselves: drinking more, smoking, taking prescription drugs (when we don't need them), using illegal drugs, eating excessively, fasting excessively, using offensive language more often, lying more often, avoiding sensitive topics of conversation, stealing, gossiping, shopping more, exercising more or less often, or exhibiting violent behavior. We could also begin to self-mutilate, neglect our personal hygiene, cook more or less, clean more or less, work more or less, surround ourselves with the wrong people, create chaotic situations, overspend, even traveling and having wonderful adventures can be a way that we cope with denial.

Denial can also be beautiful because it allows us to keep our ideals, moral values, biases, beliefs, perspectives, attitudes, and habitual behaviors intact, all of which are results of the environments we are exposed to. These can be thought of as our ego, intellect, social identity, or conscious mind. This is the part of us that adapts as it learns what is socially acceptable in the environments we find ourselves in.

The Vanity of Denial

Living in denial can allow us to continue to hold ourselves in high esteem in relation to other individuals. We appear to compartmentalize our lives and live in a manner that is fragmented and limits us in many ways. For instance, we may have plenty of friends and good times, but have very little money to support our families or us. We may have plenty of money, but have unhealthy habits resulting in toxic relationships or an unhealthy body. We can continue living this way because we can disconnect who we believe we are from what we do in each area of our lives. What we say and do has been divided into two halves that were once united. We are disjoined, but unaware of our disconnection...our double life...our contradictions...our hypocritical behavior. This makes it easier for us to, for instance, work as a healthcare provider and smoke or engage in other unhealthy habits; establish ourselves as an advocate for peace and equality, yet con people out of thousands of dollars at the same time; worship at church on Saturday or Sunday and go to work Monday morning and pollute the atmosphere with words of hate and intolerance; or enjoy a job or career in which we plan and enact systems, policies, and laws that result in polluting our communities, our water, and our bodies leading to the deterioration or devastation of large areas of land, wildlife, and groups of people including our families or us. We can do these things living completely in denial of the results caused by our active participation. We are able to do this, because there are some factors that take priority over what we see as less important or unnecessary to us at the time. We can't see the connection between them or the disconnection within us. The results we witness become completely separate from what we do.

Our major priorities keep our minds off of and disconnected from areas of our lives…the bigger picture. Things that may seem more important to us include making money, having notoriety, wielding power, having prestige, acquiring or maintaining a lifestyle, hiding the truth, creating beauty, or establishing a title or legacy. These priorities are not limited to the tangible. What we do stems from a desire to be loved and interpreting it as feeling needed, wanted, relevant, important, or valued in some way, shape, or form.

We may think of doing what we believe we need to as self-preservation such as our way of thinking, behaving, and operating in order to fulfill our deepest desire—a connection. When we are in denial, we learn early in life the perception we want people to have of us can be maintained if we hide behind our story...our script that we have rehearsed many times in our minds. Our story keeps the vision we have of ourselves intact, even though we know (consciously) it is not the truth. We can still feel good about ourselves. We imagine others see us as we see ourselves in the story we have created. In other words, even though we know the story we tell ourselves and others is not the truth, we can still feel superior to others in some area of life and continue living as we always have by saying, behaving, and doing what we have always done. During this time, we may be highly stressed because we don't want anyone to find out the truth, so on some level our mind is constantly working overtime in order to maintain the illusion. We are in denial and our ego wants to keep us there so we (it) will continue to feel in control, happy, or superior.

Question(s):

- What have you done that was totally out of character for you because of the stress you were under at the time?

- In which areas of your life are you hiding your true thoughts and feelings?
- What areas of your life don't line up with your values, morals, and idea you have of yourself?

Meet ME in DENIAL, Part 2: Poem

The director of my madness,
Her discourse overtakes my soul.
She can make me feel like a goddess
And then take me to depths I never knew existed.
She is often the opinion I cling to in the morning
And the utterance I despise at night.
He works toward her goal, ceaselessly
To permeate my thoughts
With her interpretation of my encounters.
She conceals, suppresses, and rejects my truth,
Yet also wants to help me any way she can.
She believes she knows
What is best for me.
He is so efficient at his job that she
Makes me believe her vision is my vision.
The emotions I feel from the stories

He tells me, adds a layer of credibility
That wins me over,
And lowers my guard.
There are some who have escaped her influence,
Many cracked, some broken;
Nevertheless, all heroes to those of us who are still
Controlled by her narrative.
By being aware, determined, and diligent,
I have lived to experience her intent,
Played out in perfect synchronicity
And have emerged with more wisdom and strength
Than I thought was possible.
She is my Specter Orator with a hypnotic voice,
Apparition physician
Wearing an extra sensitive stethoscope,
My shadow friend who keeps all of my secrets,
A wraith draped in a lovely translucent cloak
We shopped for, together,
And I, undeniably, captivated.

- Angela Taylor

"Things which matter most must never be at the mercy of things which matter least."
- Goethe

Chapter 3

The Denial Agency

Deny has opened her own agency in her effort to defeat our Truth. She decided to open the agency after an important mission led by Truth was compromised because Deny chose to ignore his orders instead of following the plan given by his director, Truth. Deny thought she was right in making that decision even though it caused the mission to collapse and she refused to take responsibility for the outcome. Out of indignation, Deny left the agency. Now Deny has made it her mission to spread her denials far and wide opposing Truth at every turn.

Deny never sleeps and thinks she is in control of every situation, but she knows the real truth, while trying to renounce and hide from herself...Truth will always prevail because Truth is much more intelligent, quicker, stronger, and more powerful than Deny could ever be.

I let Deny and his agents infiltrate my thoughts, which left me feeling helpless, sad, angry, frustrated, unmotivated, confused, unloved, and disconnected from others. This gave Deny control momentarily over what I experienced in my life. Her influence may be short-lived, but she's extremely effective.

When I open my heart and mind to my Truth, I have a free flow of wisdom. This wisdom is constant, consistent, accurate, and proves to be effective in influencing my life. It affords me the chance to feel love, have peace, and know joy again. This flow of wisdom is organic and a natural, health-promoting, inspirational, dynamic, and energizing flow of vitality that continues to replenish, restore, and revitalize my entire being.

I think of Truth and Deny as my executive assistants. They work inside my mind to manage my thoughts and promote what they stand for by either hiding my fears and creating stories to support them or encouraging me to honor my truth and live authentically. When I choose to let Deny assist me, I cover my truth with lies. When I have Truth as my assistant, I am honest and feel free. Whether I hire Truth or Deny to assist me, every thought I have affects my choices and ultimately influences my life. These thoughts tend to take control of my mind either by allowing me to love my life, other people, and myself, or hate/curse my life, other people, and myself.

All of that said, I now understand that when I find myself repeating a story in my head contrary to my truth, no matter what label I have slapped on it, I have been taken over by Deny and her stories of denial.

Here's a way for you to check for denials or stories Deny tells you. Ask yourself:
- How do I know the answer I have just heard is true?
- Did the thought come from someone or something in my environment?

- Does this information serve to expand or limit me in any way?
- Will it help someone else?
- Did the person or other source want to influence their agenda?
- What is their agenda? Do I agree with it?
- Does this information connect me with people and cause me to feel a bond or kinship with other people outside of the group or does it cause me to want to hide things, tell lies, or exclude others?
- Does this information make me feel disconnected, set apart, better or worse than others, or negative in any way?
- Will the information help other people or me in situations or circumstances with beneficial or harmful results in any way or to anyone?

If you ask yourself these questions and the results of your actions would be favorable for all concerned, then that is probably your truth. If not, it is more than likely a denial disguised as your truth.

Deny Enjoys Her Profession

Deny's objectives are all the same—determine what we want hidden and create the best stories (denials) for us to tell ourselves and everyone else in our lives in order to make us feel better. These stories help keep our truths safely tucked away, suppress our fears, console our egos, help regain our composure, choose an appropriate mask for us to wear in public, and continue handling our daily responsibilities and maintaining our routine. Deny's image, along with her denials, can change in an instant. She takes her cues from our thoughts and emotions and adjusts the report to form stories to give us what we need in that moment. He has the charisma, competence, and authority of a commander and his counterpart the elegance, intelligence, and poise of a queen. She is the director of all missions and has denial agents at his command ready for action to spread her denials and conceal any traces of our truths.

When is Deny in Control?

Deny and her agents may be running our lives when we feel like a victim. It may seem like one or more areas of our lives are in total chaos and we don't know how it got that way or what to do to get out of it.

If you feel as if a battle is going on inside of you emotionally or mentally, Deny is probably at the center of it. He is trying desperately to do his job by suppressing your truth and creating stories for you to hide behind, to continue spreading her beautiful denials and corrupting your thoughts all in the name of love.

Deny has control:

- When we know the truth about someone, but want to believe the best about him or her so we ignore what we know, hoping their behavior will change.
- When we are oblivious to our behavior, but our behavior is affecting our lives adversely in the form of unhealthy relationships, unfavorable business decisions, loss of money/financial wealth, poor health, angry outbursts, violence, sadness, frustration, ...
- When we are aware of how our behavior is affecting our lives, but we deny it, or we blame

other people or circumstances for our behavior or the condition of our lives.

- When we know something unfortunate or traumatic has happened to us or someone else, but choose to ignore it.
- When we have experienced something traumatic, but bury the memory of it to the point where we don't consciously remember it (suppression).
- When we are aware of our behavior, but because of pride or high self-image, we tell ourselves our behavior is acceptable.
- When we are in shock and immediately deny what is or has occurred (death of a loved one or other loss) after hearing of the news.
- When we have an issue, challenge, or habit adversely affecting our lives and possibly those around us, but we refute its existence or think we have it under control.
- When we are aware something is not working (relationship, career choice, diet, etc.), but decide to ignore our truth in hopes we are wrong, circumstances may change, or will disappear altogether.

- When we know something is not right/ appropriate for us, but we engage in it anyway believing it will be worth our gain.

- When we are aware something is not right/ appropriate for us, but we fear what might happen if we acknowledge it or attempt to change it.

- When we know something is potentially dangerous, against the law, hazardous to our health or someone else's, painful or even fatal, but pretend it is not a big deal.

- When we regress to earlier stages of development as a reaction to situations that may become too overwhelming to deal with.

- When we suppress negative or destructive thoughts and feelings consciously, but do something inappropriate or out of the ordinary to release the emotions we feel. In case of children, they may not know how to express what they are feeling.

- When our self-image is of one who is honest, yet we take things without asking (steal), cheat on our taxes, tell lies to get what we want, we are unconscious of the duality.

- When our self-image is of one who is moral, kind, and compassionate, yet we willingly—mentally, emotionally, and/or physically—hurt or harm others who are different or express views that oppose our own and we are unconscious of the conflicting values.

- When we project our thoughts or feelings onto someone else because we feel uncomfortable or do not think it is right for us to express such thoughts and feelings.

- When we don't really like someone, but go out of our way to be extra nice to show we really like him or her.

- When we have repressed an emotionally disturbing memory in an effort to continue our daily life.

- When we are frustrated or angry with someone, but feel it is unsafe to express it to that person and, instead, take it out on someone else who we may feel is subordinate in some way.

This is by no means a complete list. This list is meant to give you some insight into how denial might be on display in our lives.

Who Does Deny Control?

No one is immune to Deny's charms. She is patient and methodical, knowing exactly what to do and say to persuade us to hire her to help our pain go away. She wants us to listen to her *instead* of our truth. Deny gets to all of us at one time or another; just when we let our guard down, she finds a way in. Nevertheless, she can be defeated when we begin listening to our truth. Truth can pull us out of any denial because her words run deep and her voice can be heard even when Deny is narrating her (Deny's) stories.

Deny may be controlling those of us who:
- May not like change.
- May not like confrontation.
- May not care about the consequences of actions.
- May not want to hurt others feelings.
- May want to hurt other people.

- May feel trapped.
- May enjoy drama we create in our life.
- May not know how to make change happen.
- May be living a life to make others happy.
- May be exhibiting addictive behavior in an effort to numb emotions or escape reality. These behaviors can be associated with denial.
- May be stressed out, angry, frustrated, fearful, sad, dissatisfied with your life, withdrawn, have anxiety attacks, depressed, overwhelmed, exhausted...
- May not feel any joy, peace, happiness, relaxation, love, or fun—feel good emotions.
- May not have a close friend or confidant.
- May be having the same challenges repeatedly.
- May keep attracting negative people into your life.
- May fear bodily harm or ridicule from others.
- May fear abandonment.

- May fear incarceration.
- May fear losing a loved one or relationship.
- May fear losing our lifestyle.
- May be willing to risk all to have what we desire.
- May have maxed out credit cards.
- May be unable to pay bills due to overspending.
- May be in the process of or have filed bankruptcy.
- May have no savings due to overspending.
- May be living paycheck to paycheck.
- May have been told that some attitude, behavior, or habit needs to change in order to earn a promotion, reach a goal, feel better, be pain free, have more money, live a better life, have peace of mind, etc., but refuses to acknowledge it.
- May know we need to alter a behavior, but feel unable to change it.
- May have said, "But, I don't want to do that," knowing we really need to.

- May have a high self-image, but may be making choices in direct conflict with our image, so we hide the truth.
- May keep getting into trouble or our loved ones continue to get into trouble (possibly children), but refuse to acknowledge that we or they are doing anything to cause it (victims of circumstance).
- May fear losing a position, job, or career.
- May fear appearing weak.
- May feel superior or inferior to other groups or individuals.
- May be suicidal.
- May be unwilling, unmotivated, or uninspired to make changes.
- May not want to get out of bed because of overwhelming feelings caused by our circumstances.
- May have temper tantrums (throw things, punch the wall or people, fight, break things), in response to overwhelming emotions usually suppressed in what may seem like inappropriate situations.

- May cut ourselves to express physically what we feel emotionally.
- May accuse a friend of gossiping when we are the one that gossips.
- May be extraordinarily helpful, nice, and accommodating to someone we don't really like.
- May have buried the memory of a tragic accident or incident, without having the ability to recall it at all.

Examine every aspect of your life.
- Are you prospering in every area?
- Where does Deny reign supreme?
- What are your challenges?
- What are the denials Deny is hiding for you?
- What are the stories behind your denials?
- What is your truth?

Denial Melodrama: Poem

I am living in a world concealed...a story protected,
A dream impersonating my life,
Performed between dimensions.
One day I will write a play, a one-woman show.
I will leave room for embellishment to make the script
more palpable—my truth, silent between the lines.
The script is written for my audience,
The spectators of my life.
In my story, I am the writer, the lead actor,
And the supporting actor. I am the producer,
Director, financier, cameraman, and
I own the recording studio where I arrange the music
Accompanying this fable.
Line by line I say with emotion. Superficiality unbroken.
They don't understand it is just a fabrication, letters,
Words, and phrases put together.
It is about my life they believe,

The height, the length, and the depth of it.
Only I know what is hidden behind the camera,
The cinematography of the phantom world,
What the lyrics say when the music is played backward.
The chants, screams, cries, and whimpers
Imperceptible, captured by their souls, yet unaware.
The disordered maze between the notes in the score
Of music I provide originated inside of the melodrama
Performed with perfection, until my lines and lyrics
Float away on air escaping to the underworld,
And drift into oblivion.
I bring a quasi-authentic portrayal of myself
To this rhythmical liturgy and its cadence camouflages
My life behind the screen.

- Angela Taylor

"In order to change the world, you have to get your head together first."
- Jimi Hendrix

Chapter 4

Wading Through Our Denials

"For the good that I would I do not:
but the evil which I would not, that I do."
The Apostle Paul (Romans 7:19)

We often don't do what we know we should, but why? We have unimaginable quantities of information at our fingertips. This generation is the most knowledgeable and tech savvy, yet with all of the information in the world at our disposal, which could serve to assist us in feeling, being, and living better, we continue to partake in unhealthy living. We stay in relationships that aren't right for us; we overeat and consume nutrient deficient foods; we fail to exercise appropriately to become fitter or maintain our health. We push people away when we want them to stay, lose job after job or quit because we don't want to acknowledge our issues, continue to spend and buy things on credit though it puts us in a deeper financial hole. We don't attend church often, but when we do, we leave feeling more encouraged; we continue buying things that we know won't satisfy the need we're trying to fill. We refuse to change. Why? Why do we often crave change, but don't make change happen, even when we know what to do? I know…easy, comfortable, and safe, but let's go a little deeper. If we want change, it's important to be aware of what's really happening.

Mantras, Intellect, and Emotions

I was forced to look at my denials and become more aware of my thoughts and behavior. I moved in with my mom when I separated from my husband. I harbored bitterness toward my mom because my thoughts about her stemming from my childhood up to that point were in a loop that replayed old situations and negative emotions, keeping me in that bitter state.

After I was at her home for a while, I added new things to be bitter about to my already long list. Obviously, she also had a list because while I was there, we both complained about each other and seemed irritated by the other's actions. I realized we were both continuing this cycle by repeating the same statements (mantras) over and over, every day...several times a day. She had hers and I had mine and it kept us in a negative feedback loop. Of course, I saw her pattern before I saw mine and since I noticed her mantras first, I told her about them. Then, I had to look at myself and examine the things I had been thinking (to myself) and feeling about her behavior, her mantras, and my responses to her mantras. Soon I began to notice that everyone who came into the household had negative mantras we were all repeating, which were in direct contrast to how we wanted to interact with each other. These mantras were keeping us in a state of confusion, frustration, and anger. Mantra, as I am using it here means: a word or phrase that is repeated often or that expresses someone's basic beliefs (www.merriam-webster.com).

I saw the patterns of behavior in everyone around me for years, but had not examined my own. I realized that what I thought was ill will towards me was just a general pattern of behavior. Their behavior had nothing to do with me at all. I found that every person had a pattern of thoughts that had become habitual. The patterns corresponded to emotions triggered by words, facial expressions, body language, attitudes, behavior, etc.

Before that, I blamed everyone else for the health of my relationships with them. By blaming everyone else, I could let myself off the hook (stay in denial) and not even see how my behavior affected my relationships.

I realized I saw everyone through a veil of conceit. It made me feel superior somehow to know they had issues that I could see (while denying my own), not knowing at the same time the issues I saw in them were the ones I couldn't see in myself. Once I realized all of the confusion I felt inside that manifested into our present reality was coming from my perceptions, I had a shift in my thinking. This changed my feelings about each person. I realized we all developed patterns of behavior that served us in some way. I began to feel empathy for the people in my life and had to forgive myself for blaming them for the conditions of our relationship by taking responsibility for my attitudes and behaviors contributing to the state my relationships with them were in.

The thought patterns created may have resulted in an outcome that benefited us at an earlier point in life, but do not serve us well in the present. The patterns developed as a consequence of our limited, individual, yet intimately personal, perception of our world. I now understand these patterns need to evolve and change as we gain more knowledge and experience and it is important to apply what we've learned to our lives.

Many times what we learn, stays in our intellect (as acquired knowledge) and is not applied to our lives for us to experience the knowledge in a personal way. When we are living in denial, what we know and how we feel can be in conflict. This lack of continuity between our thinking and feeling can hinder our progress. Applying our knowledge and combining it with what we learn through our emotional experiences, can transform into wisdom. This is when we grow to understand the knowledge on a deeper level. For instance, it's easy to say that in order to lose weight people should eat right and exercise; however, when we have experienced the emotional and psychological turmoil that sometimes comes with losing weight, we can offer advice that may help someone overcome some of the obstacles in their path. Some of these experiences could be: losing weight and gaining it back, buying exercise gadgets that lose their thrill, trying fad diets that don't work, expending the time and energy it takes to prepare the proper meals and exercising appropriately, and knowing how it feels to lack the motivation, determination, and the will it takes to reach those goals. We know there are emotional and psychological challenges to be considered before diet and exercise is factored in. Why? Due to our intellect and emotions influencing everything we do, the knowledge and deeper understanding of what it takes to lose weight and keep it off may then be able to help someone else who had the same issues with losing weight. We understand, not only the practical components needed to work in sync to reach a weight loss goal, but also the thoughts and emotions a person may experience, which may allow us to be more effective in helping them lose weight. Expressing empathy can make a difference. Ignoring this reality is living in denial.

I watched a reality show once in which a health and fitness expert lived with a family for a period of time. There was a teenage girl in the home who had some emotional issues, however, she was also overweight. The fitness professional zeroed in on the girl's lack of exercise as being the problem and never empathized with her situation. I could see the teen wanted to discuss her situation, but she didn't feel empowered; however, the fitness trainer overlooked her mental and emotional condition and was not able to make a connection with the girl. After receiving an exercise program, the girl walked away disappointed. I don't know whether she used the program or not, but my point is it is important to be able to empathize with people (meet them where they are) in order for us to even begin to help them or understand them, in order for us to assist with taking them where they need to be. The fitness professional was not a psychologist and counseling her would have been beyond her scope of practice. That is not what I am suggesting, though I do believe if she had just listened to what the teen had to say, she may have been able to make some suggestions that could have inspired her to move beyond her barriers to exercise in order for her to begin to embrace a new lifestyle.

Understanding that our bodies are important and our intellect and emotions are also vital parts that make us who we are is of the utmost importance; otherwise it is easy for us to neglect one in favor of the other. When we do, an adult can end up with a healthy, muscle-bound or well-conditioned body and the mind and emotions of an adolescent, living the stories of denial and wondering why areas of their lives are in turmoil.

Question(s):

- What do you hear yourself say about a person, event, situation, or circumstance most of the time? This is your mantra.

- How does your mantra make you feel after you have stated it? Is it an emotion you want to continue feeling?

- Is your mantra something you want to continue experiencing in your life?

- Are you so focused on a healthy body that you neglect your intellectual and emotional wellbeing?

- What are you doing presently to make sure your mind and emotions are receiving the nourishment they need in order to remain healthy and strong?

- What does being healthy and strong in mind and emotions mean to you?

Who is this Person: Poem

I don't recognize her.
She's wakes up in my bed every morning,
Or is it hers?
I don't know because when she gets up
And I stand in the mirror
It's her reflection I see, not mine.
After I shower, right before I brush my teeth
When I look in the mirror to examine them,
I see her again, not me.
Who is she and what has she done with me?
How did I get inside of her shell?
It feels like it might be a prison cell
I don't know how to get out
Am I thinking her thoughts or is she thinking mine?
Are my ideas my own, or hers?
Does she visualize the same future I see for myself?
How did I get here? Is there anyone who can tell me,
Help me understand, if I am her and she is me,
Whose life are we living?
It must be hers. It couldn't be mine.
It doesn't fit me, feels a size too small

And her body is two sizes too large.
The people she hangs out with
I don't understand,
And they don't seem to understand me.
The atmosphere of my surroundings
Feels uncomfortable like the tight pants
She tries to fit into.
I don't belong here, so why am I?
I want someone else to be security
In this store where this mannequin lives.
I don't want to be her eyes anymore.
I want my own body and store.
I want to be my own eyes in the sky.
I want free reign in my own body.
I want to look out and see myself.
I want the atmosphere around me to feel right,
Not confining and suffocating.
How do I get out of this suit I'm wearing?
Do I tell her I need to meditate tonight?
Will she listen?
Do I tell her I need to pray and get some inspiration?
How can I get through to her
To let her know I'm here,
That I want my own home?
I'll ask her if we can pray tonight and after we do
I'll get a good night's sleep and dream of my own roof.
When I look in the mirror tomorrow,
I hope to see me again
And not look out into a foreign land.

- Angela Taylor

Chapter 5

Deny and Our Default Settings

Even though we may be working to change, grow, learn, and behave differently, we sometimes fall back to our default settings. We all have default settings. They consist of all of the information we have assimilated throughout the years—what we have learned and accepted as our truth absorbed from the environments we were exposed to as we grew into adulthood. It includes everything we were taught by the people around us as we learned how to navigate through the world. Deny's stories of denial handed down to us from family members, friends, co-workers, neighbors, the news, advertising, social media, etc., can infiltrate and distort our truths until at some point we realize our lives are in shambles. We may often find ourselves in the middle of some chaotic situation...usually angry with someone or frequently sad or hurt by others' words and actions. We may even be frustrated and stressed out most of the time without knowing why.

Often, what we want out of life and how we want to be are in direct contrast with our default setting. If our default setting says, "All men are dogs, all black people are lazy, all rich people are thieves, all poor people are hapless, all white people are racist and none of them can be trusted," we are acting according to what our default setting tells us, which again, is based on what we have learned from our environments. However, when we learn new information and it conflicts with our old patterns of belief, what happens to the new information? We can either deny the new information or apply the new information to our lives and begin to think, and behave, according to our new perspective.

Sometimes our default setting is so ingrained and deeply rooted into our psyche it may take almost a lifetime to finally accept our truth and apply it to our lives. Some people never change no matter how often they hear a different perspective; they deny it and continue living their lives guided by their default setting. For example, what if you want to find a good man or woman to marry, but you believe all males or females are trouble? Let's say you only see what you believe to be true (your perspective); what kind of men or women will you attract into your life? You will more than likely attract one that reflects what you know to be true. If you do find someone you believe to be a good person, but your belief about men and women hasn't changed, you will treat him or her according to your perspective...as trouble. You may hear yourself say over and over with each break-up that you knew he/she was trouble from the beginning or you always knew he/she would do something to ruin the relationship. It is also easy to blame the other person because nobody is perfect. We each come with a history of residue called issues or challenges we need to work through.

We may experience these scenarios because of the insecurity created by the experiences we have acquired during our life, which has been reinforced by our default setting. Another example may be your girlfriends are getting married one after another to good men (according to their definition of a good man). Your girlfriends tell you good men are out there you just have to know it. You retort by saying, "There are no good men left!" You flatly deny what they are saying. You tell your friends they will see the truth when their men turn out to be the losers you always knew they were. Years pass and your girlfriends are happy and enjoying their lives with their new loves, but you can't understand it and believe their time is coming because to you, all men are losers. Years go by and one or two of your girlfriends may have divorced, but the others' marriages are still going strong and seem to be healthy, loving, and nurturing. Your love life on the other hand is in shambles because you just can't seem to find "a good man;" the ones you've dated have all been losers. What do you do? Do you continue to let Deny control your life? Do you listen and make an effort to internalize a different perspective of men because you see evidence of it by observing your girlfriends in their relationship with their husbands?   Do you continue operating by what your default setting is telling you or do you begin to create a new default setting?

My Denial Default Settings

We have created a default setting for every area of our lives.   Here are the 8 Areas of the Circle of Life as listed in the book, *Breathe in God's Love & Light* by Walter L. Beckley.   With this, I am listing my general negative default settings along with the ongoing dialogue that I am either in the process of changing and replacing or have changed and replaced.   As you read through my list, ask yourself what yours might be. The answers may surprise you.

The 8 Areas of the Circle of Life

1. Body Default Setting

Default Dialogue: Diet/Fat Release

"Eating these cookies isn't going to hurt.   At least I'm not eating ten with each sitting.   I'm hungry and I want something good to eat.   I'm going to get what I want and enjoy it!   I deserve to treat myself.   I need to hold my stomach in so people can't see how big it really is.   I know I need to eat more nutritious foods, but I have no control when it comes to chocolate chip cookies. I ate well yesterday; I can eat what I want to today."

My Truth: It's important for me to eat more nutritious meals. It's important for me to cut back on foods loaded with refined sugar and snack on more fruits and vegetables instead. Eating whatever I want whenever I want and as much as I want causes excess fat around my middle, butt, and thighs that does not look attractive to me. When I eat better quality and nutrient dense foods, I feel better and I maintain a healthy weight with the addition of appropriate exercise.

Default Dialogue: Skin irritation, acid reflux, hair breakage, night sweats

- *Skin Irritation*: "I don't know what is causing this itching, so in the meantime I'm going to enjoy the foods I like. These cookies may be causing the itching, but I'm going to eat them…they're really good. I really want some soda. I could go for a chocolate cupcake right now. I know I have probably had too much sugar today, but I'll eat this cookie tonight and cut back tomorrow. The food I'm eating isn't causing the itching. Maybe it's the moisturizer I use, although I have been using it for years."

- *Acid Reflux*: The ENT specialist told me to stop eating chocolate (not going to happen, can't live without a little chocolate in my life); garlic (but I put garlic in almost everything I cook. It brings the flavor to life); beverages with caffeine (but I really like Cherry Pepsi); acidic fruits (but I have just started making fresh lemonade with fresh strawberries), and onions. I don't believe having these things less and in smaller quantities will hurt me. My favorite chocolate chip cookies are not going anywhere. I have to have my cookies."

- *Night sweats*: "The changes that my body goes through each month is what I think is causing the night sweats."

- *Hair breakage:* "I believe it is the perm causing dryness and breakage of my hair. I have been perming my hair for years."

- *Insomnia:* "I am just excited about what is going on in my life right now."

- *Excessive sleeping:* "I heard napping is good."

- *Nightmares:* "I shouldn't have eaten right before I went to bed last night."
- *Pneumonia:* "I have never had pneumonia before; I guess it had to catch up with me at some point."
- *Anxiety Attacks:* "I have been doing too much lately. I just need to cut back on some of my responsibilities and get more rest."
- *Shingles:* "I thought only old people got shingles."

My truth: It would be best for me to stop eating so much junk food; I should decrease my over consumption of acidic foods, including chocolate if I want acid reflux symptoms to decrease and diminish; it would be best for me to pay more attention to my diet and the products I am using on my skin; the stress I am under is more than likely causing my hair breakage and I cannot deal with the issues I am facing that are at the root of my stress; I am dealing with symptoms of stress.

2. Mental Default Setting

Denial Default Dialogue

See above and add: "What is wrong with me? I feel like I keep going around in circles. I'm not accomplishing, moving, solving anything, gaining any ground, feeling any better, releasing any fat or improving, and I don't understand why. I don't want to do that (fear)."

My Truth: The answers that I need are always here. I just need to get quiet enough to hear them.

3. Emotional Default Setting

Denial Default Dialogue

"I don't know why I feel frustrated. Why do I feel so angry? I feel stressed...anxious, but I don't know why. He, she, and/or they make me so angry. I shouldn't feel so overwhelmed. When he, she, and/or they do that, it makes me so angry and I don't know why. That doesn't bother me (but it really does). That is ok (but it really isn't). What he, she, and/or they said or did didn't affect me (but it did)."

My truth: It is ok for me to feel emotion, even those I think are negative. It is important for me to acknowledge my feelings and express them in an appropriate manner. It is my responsibility to examine and determine why I feel negatively towards an individual, behavior, situation, circumstance, words, attitudes, or group, so I can understand myself better, grow, manage my emotions better, and maintain a more peaceful state of being.

4. Relationships Default Setting

<u>Denial Default Dialogue</u>

"I don't understand people. People are mean and selfish. I don't like people because they are mean to me. People don't seem to like me. It's hard to make friends. People usually end up hurting me in some way."

"What if it doesn't work? What if I'm wrong about him, her, and/or them? What if they reject me? They may not like me. It's their fault that I _____. It's because of my experiences in childhood that I _____. It's because of my experiences in childhood that I don't _____. It's because of my parents that I _____."

My truth: I am responsible for my own happiness, the condition of my relationships, and my life.

5. Financial Default Setting

Denial Default dialogue

"What am I going to do? The money I need isn't in my accounts. I don't have anything in my wallet. How am I going to buy groceries and pay my bills? My credit cards are almost maxed out. What am I going to do? I don't have enough to pay for everything."

My truth: It is important for me to learn how to manage my money more effectively, make more money to manage, spend less on non-essential items, create a savings budget, and in addition, begin investing my money wisely.

6. Career/Lifestyle Default Setting

Denial Default Dialogue

"I don't know if I am ready for _____. I don't know if I have enough knowledge yet. I don't know whether I can do that. I don't know whether I have enough experience for that. I don't know if I am capable of being successful. I don't want to be perceived as incompetent. I don't want to look foolish. What if I can't do it? What if they won't accept it? What if they don't like me? What if I don't like it? What if I make mistakes? I don't know if I'm _____ enough. I don't know if I will be able to achieve all that I envision for myself. What if I fall short of my dreams? Am I being unrealistic?"

My truth: I can have, do, and be anything I know I can. The only restrictions are the ones I see for myself. It is important for me to work for what I want in life and not blame anyone or anything for the condition my life.

7. Spiritual Default Setting

Denial Default Dialogue

"I need to pray and meditate more. I need to attend church regularly."

My truth: I can get inspiration from attending Sunday morning worship services, being in nature, reading an inspirational book, listening to positive affirmations, and talking with people who are inspired. I can become aware of my connection to the creator whenever I want to. I create a relationship with my higher power by acknowledging God, being aware of a connection on a regular basis, and listening to the Spirit's guidance. I am always connected and only need to slow down, become aware of my connection, get quiet, and breathe deeply, which is also what I do as I meditate.

8. Energy Default Setting

<u>Denial Default Dialogue</u>

"I need to push myself a little bit more so that I can complete _____. I have to keep working through lunch so that I can achieve _____. I can't be tired; I haven't done anything...I'm not really tired. I probably just need to eat. I don't know why I feel exhausted. I can't be tired; I have too much left to do! I feel a little frustrated and stressed, but I can't slow down now. I never feel comfortable around them, but maybe it is just me; I don't feel comfortable in those situations and I don't understand why. I feel drained after talking to her on the phone, but she's my friend; I can't just stop talking to her."

My truth: It is important for me to take a break when I feel like I need it. My mind and body acknowledges when I need to slow down and rest. My body may not be active all day, but my mind is always working and needs some down time.   It is ok to relax, breathe, revitalize, recuperate, sleep, vacation, close my eyes, meditate, and find a quiet place to unwind, have fun, nurture, and enjoy my relationships.

Think about your default settings.

Question(s):

- What are your default settings?

- What is your default dialogue?

- What is your truth?

Denial in the House: Poem

Saw you wearing your friend's shirt,
Seemed odd.
Saw him look at you a certain way,
I think he had too much to drink.
Were you holding hands at the table before I walked in?
I imagined it.
Comes along to celebrate our anniversary,
A little peculiar.
Heard him in the background telling you to come back,
Said you were working late.
He began to act resentful,
Thought we were friends.
I asked the children if they would like to stay with you
While I'm on my business trip.
They cried out, "We want to stay with you, mom!"
I think they misunderstood.
You're taking a guy's weekend away again?
OK, have a great time!

- Angela Taylor

"It is necessary to keep one's compass in one's eyes and not in the hand, for the hands execute, but the eye judges."

- Michelangelo

Chapter 6

Under Cover Denials

Deny, with her list of denials helps us duck, dodge, and hide <u>from</u> our truth. She doesn't diminish our truth. Our truth is ALWAYS there just waiting to be revealed, brought to light, uncovered, discovered, acknowledged, voiced, and lived. Like new discoveries made in science, we know more now than ever before about the universe, our world, and our bodies. Scientists are forever looking, waiting, watching, analyzing, hypothesizing, and performing experiments to reveal answers to questions previously asked. Throughout history some scientists died while in the process of trying to solve a mystery or have been killed because they were close to discovering the answers to an age-old question before the powers that be were ready to hear it.

History reveals when one scientist in his or her lifetime doesn't make the discovery he or she worked so diligently to achieve, another scientist, or team of scientists, in the next generation or two pick up where it was left off and continue until the discovery is made, the equation completed, or the experiment performed in which the outcome results in an answer transporting science forward.

As a caveat, it blows my mind how the next generation takes the baton and runs farther than the previous one and it continues to happen with each generation. We are amazing creations and continue to advance beyond what the previous generations had ever imagined.

At times, our truth in her quietness gets pushed aside by Deny with her sweet words of solace. Deny's persuasion allows us to keep the perks we receive by applying her extensive repertoire of denials. We often use her inventory to cover up what we don't want others to know. Now, more than ever before, I hear myself say, "People never cease to amaze me." Most often this occurs when I'm on Facebook watching a video someone sent with a person saying or doing something unimaginable, yet it is funny, normal, and interesting to the person posting it, if only to entertain the unsuspecting viewer. People are showing sides of themselves that before social media and reality television programs they wouldn't be caught dead saying or doing. What they reveal can uncover the stories of denials they have decided to employ in order to help them navigate through their lives.

Risky Denials

Some of us like to live on the edge. If something is exciting and a little dangerous it's like eating our favorite candy—the more we have, the more we want. Being venturous and a little naughty once in a while can make life interesting, fun, less predictable, and less hazardous when appropriate safeguards are considered. This can include everything from wearing leather gear and a helmet while riding a motorcycle, texting after you have reached your destination and parked the car, all the way to taking precautions when anticipating a romantic encounter or impromptu rendezvous.

Maybe you like to walk on the wild side while feeling the wind on your face. You know you are the exception to every rule. You are grown and sexy and can do whatever you please. You may even give yourself a title like *Free Spirit*, *Daredevil*, or *Independent Woman*. Deny can encourage you to do things that seem like an exhilarating challenge or exciting encounter and before you know it, you're in a mess up to your eyeballs, or at the very least embarrassed as heck.

Deny's voice can be intoxicating. She beckons to us because she really wants to help us get what we want. She does not judge or criticize. She just does what she does best...suppress feelings we want to avoid using the stories she whispers to us. So, enticed by her stories of fun and adventure, we choose to follow the charming dialogue of Deny and avoid thoughts about consequences resulting from our risky behavior. Be careful and look both ways before crossing the street;

Denial can make you feel like you are floating through air on the way to your destination one moment and wondering what happened the next.

Why Experience is the Best Teacher

"Until we encounter a situation personally, we may only understand it intellectually and therefore may be unmotivated to acknowledge it, but when it affects our lives…impacts our minds…interrupts the natural flow of our day…causes an effect in our relationships, finances, etc., we immediately feel the <u>emotional</u> impact of the situation. The effect has interrupted our thoughts and behaviors in the present and subsequently influences the results we encounter. <u>Feeling</u> it can prompt us to act, get involved, speak up, help someone, get out of our comfort zone, change things, or make a difference. This call to action is activated in a deeper place—from living (experiencing) it on a deeper level.

Acknowledging the possibilities in life (not being afraid of them) helps to keep us out of denial. Being proactive instead of reactive creates a level of comfort and peace that we otherwise only wish we had."

- Angela Taylor

The Top of Denial: Discrimination

There is another undercover denial prevalent in our world today: discrimination. We discriminate in many ways about many things. In fact, we discriminate every single day in every moment by choosing one thing that is better compared to another. However, what I am writing about here is when a person, or group of people, is treated differently from people with whom we may share basic commonalities. These commonalities can be anything from race, gender, belief systems, communities, and religious ideologies, to being employed by the same organization, corporation, or company with people we interact with every day. Of course these common bonds also include intrinsic bonds such as familial attitudes, biases, and beliefs. These commonalities create a psychological and emotional connection allowing us to accept small and large infractions from those who discriminate because the common bond shared takes precedence over any behavior exhibited. We, in essence, feel more for those with whom we share a bond than those we don't. This sometimes allows us to deny the discrimination we may witness and instead rationalize the behavior of those who discriminate. We may even deny that discrimination exists.

Discrimination can also be overlooked or disregarded because when people discriminate they are not on the receiving end of the discrimination and therefore are not affected by it in a way that decreases their self-esteem. They have no point of reference in which to categorize it and no emotions that coincide with it because they cannot relate to how the person on the receiving end feels. They cannot empathize with others who have experienced it, nor can they grasp the fact that some people may experience discrimination every day of their lives in subtle ways, the same ways in which they choose to discriminate. This may not be a big deal to the discriminator because he or she does not have skin in the game...so to speak. This makes it easy for discrimination to exist and persist. It also makes it easy to dismiss as a figment of the imagination of the person being discriminated against. Even when discrimination is evident, its existence can still be denied. In his book, *Why Do I Do That,* Joseph Burgo writes, "We usually go through life believing our conscious experience of ourselves is the beginning and end of who we are, in truth, important parts of our emotional lives may remain hidden from us." Is there another version of you lurking in the darkest corners of your mind who only comes out when a certain emotion is triggered?

If you have been discriminated against for one reason in particular, when you think about discrimination, that reason is what will come to mind first. For example, for people of color the initial thought could be discrimination based solely on race or ethnicity, which is pervasive, especially in the United States, but unfortunately is not limited to its borders.

Discrimination comes in many forms. We can even experience discrimination from people who share our race or culture. We can be discriminated against because of the color or shade of our skin or texture of our hair, thickness of our lips, shape of our eyes, shape of our nose, our height, our body weight, our gender, how well or poorly we verbally communicate, our age or lack of experience, our style of clothing, our level of education, our financial status, where we live, our religious beliefs, the music we listen to, our lifestyle choices, our sexual preferences, where we work, our employment status, our friends or family, the lack of power or influence we are perceived to have, and any stereotype emphasizing and devaluing any unique qualities when compared to others within our own race or culture.

Denial helps us to justify our behavior by keeping the denial stories (beliefs that tell us we are right) in a position of prominence at all times. In addition to that, we tend to look for things that coincide with our perspective. Everything outside of that goes unnoticed or may be dismissed as an anomaly. It is like when you buy a new red car; suddenly you begin to notice *all* of the red cars you had not paid any attention to before. All of the other colors fade into obscurity because you are now focused on one particular color. Did the other cars just disappear because you decided to focus on one color? No.

We can discriminate against others or see discrimination occurring all around us and then wonder why the people who are discriminated against are so angry or we may think, they should just get over it.

Denying that discrimination exists when we immortalize its existence is a perfect example of denial working efficiently undercover, but in plain sight.

Questions(s):

- What are the denials you can see now on a daily basis actively working in plain sight that you or others may not have been aware of?
- If you are thinking, saying, or doing things that you wouldn't want done to you, your family, or anyone you hold dear, what is the purpose of your behavior?

The Great Escape: Poem

There is an echo in this room. Furniture is sparse;
I am seated in an overstuffed couch in the center of the
Room with a matching chair
And a floor lamp to read by to its right.
There is an etched glass coffee table,
And a ceiling fan above my head
Twirling in slow motion.
There is a bar to the left of me topped with
A sky blue glass pitcher with cold ice water
And lime slices floating like lily pads on top.
My favorite libations are all lined up to tickle my tongue
Bananas, ripe mangos, ruby red cherries,
And three choices of melon are here to entice my pallet.
Cashews, walnuts, and macadamia nuts are in

Small, clear glass bowls
On the coffee table in front of me
And my go-to foods when I've had a rough day,
Complete my spread.
From the open double French doors
With panes of glass and sheer lilac curtains
suspended from the rod atop, blowing lightly
In the wind,
I can hear the ocean waves rolling up
And blending with the shore.
I hear the birds singing in the distance
As they fly above the water,
Waiting patiently for lunch
To jump from the ocean,
All under the noonday sun.
The cool breeze caresses my skin and prompts me to
Melt into the cushions of the couch.
In the air I detect freshly baked chocolate chip cookies,
Drifting in from the bakery three blocks away.
Raspberry iced tea in hand with just enough ice,
And a slice of lime on the side,
Soft music is floating in,
Chosen from my preferred playlist,
Peaceful and tranquil.
My choice of accommodation,
My getaway.
My break from the norm.
I'm not evading anything; this is my destination.
This is a cloud for my mind to float on.

- Angela Taylor

"The only real mistake is the one from which we learn nothing."

- Henry Ford

Chapter 7

What Am I Trying to Avoid?

I have learned that what I tried to avoid is what I needed to go through in order to get to the other side, get to the next step, reach my goals, experience happiness, find my peace, realize love, and enjoy my relationships and my life. There are things we must go through in order to feel better, be free, and reach our goals, however, we can spend so much time and energy trying not to go through things we waste most of our lives trying to avoid.

Mistakes are Worth Their Weight in Gold!

I spend a lot of time planning, studying, researching, practicing, asking questions, and thinking about the best course of action before I make a move to ensure I make as few mistakes as possible. I want to appear knowledgeable, efficient, competent and prepared, even when things seem to be going awry behind the scenes. Who doesn't, right? However, I have found that when I do make mistakes, they teach me a valuable lesson, show me what not to do, point me in the right direction, create an opportunity that wasn't there before, or cause me to meet or talk to someone who becomes instrumental in guiding me to better ways. Now, I won't say I welcome mistakes, but I don't dread them as much as I once did and I am more open to making them because I know there is a gold nugget at the other end.

Mistakes are a part of life. We must get over it. Most of what we see, hear, use, smell, taste, and touch may have begun as a mistake in which someone was attempting something completely different and found it worked to improve our lives in an unexpected area. Embrace your mistakes and collect the nuggets along the way.

Work Your Way Out of Denial

We may feel like we are ready for something we want, when in fact we need to have a few more experiences, challenges, or lessons before we are equipped with just what we need to make a great opportunity a successful one. Until then, we may live in denial of what we know we need because we think we are the exception to the rule. We may fool ourselves into thinking what we have is good enough, when we know it really isn't. We may deny (out of fear) that we need help, need more education, need a mentor, need to network, need to forgive, need to manage our anger, need to contain our emotions, need to change our attitude, need to talk to a therapist, need to see a doctor, need to practice, etc., before we are ready to advance to the next elevation of learning and living.

I wanted to become an entrepreneur, but didn't think I had the leadership qualities needed in order to be inspirational, effective, and successful. I was afraid of people when I was younger. I was very shy, self-conscious, and afraid to speak in front of other people or even speak up for myself. I also didn't think I had the aptitude because I thought of myself as having average intelligence and alleged only people with advanced degrees could be effective leaders. I didn't think an advanced degree was anywhere in my future, so what was I to do? I thought I needed more intellect, more personality, more courage, and the ability to cultivate good relationships with people. In addition, I was born into a middle class family; money was not set aside for me to use when I came of age. However, I really wanted to acquire what I needed in order to have an optimal career. I remember taking business courses, courses to improve my memory, and even spoke in front of groups of people, usually to read an essay or poem I wrote, but I still felt inadequate. I tried very hard to push those feelings as far down inside of my chamber as I could, as to not feel them. I chose to deny how I felt about myself and I wanted to avoid the pain I felt when I thought about not having, doing, or being enough.

I couldn't deny a personality that everyone saw and I felt and lived each day. How can I change my personality...something that is so much a part of who I am? Do I have to change who I am? How do I do that? If I do that, who will I be? Can I just fake it until I make it?   I tried that and it worked for a while, but the insecurities were still there. They were always there; my truth was covered and concealed by Deny's stories. They would call to me from my chamber of denials kept safely hidden away by Deny.   I could hear their cries, moans, and scratches from trying to claw their way out, not realizing their words could not be deciphered through the thick padding.   There was no way out unless I decided I wanted to hear what they had to say, but I did not, so there they remained restless and clamorous, one level below my conscious awareness. They were tucked away in my subconscious—or unconscious—waiting for the day when they could finally be free to feel the sunlight shining from my conscious mind, brought out into the open to be seen.   On that day, they will be animated, gracious, and delighted, jumping and clapping their hands enthusiastically.   In my imagination, I can see Deny standing near the chamber, keys and lock in one hand and the other on her hip, smiling, as the joy of my insecurities is contagious; it comes from a place that is pure. Beneath their longing is my truth, waiting to be revealed by close inspection of each denial's birth and journey. They have a long wait, years, decades to know what it will feel like to be free.

The sounds my denials made grew louder and began to invade my conscious thoughts as the years ticked by and I trudged through life. It seemed like my world came tumbling down right before I was diagnosed with depression. I could no longer hold back the cries from within my chamber. The anguish I felt on a daily basis was almost too much to bear. I thought I was holding myself together well, but I wasn't. The signs and symptoms of stress that began to manifest as physical ailments, should have been motivation enough for me to seek help to feel healthy and free again, but they weren't.

I wasn't ready to be an effective leader or start my own business when it first became a goal. I have to do the work that it will take to get to where I want to be. With each year, my experiences and mistakes are preparing me for what I need to become the leader I want to become.

Now that I am feeling much better and am recovering from what I imagine hell would feel like, I feel as though I have acquired some invaluable knowledge about myself, my connection with others, and what it feels like to feel stressed out and depressed. I have a new purpose and want to help others who have or are experiencing stress, anxiety, and depression.

I beseech you to begin to examine your life, learn more about yourself, and find out what you need to do in order to begin to recover, heal, and take advantage of the new opportunities awaiting you. I had some learning, living, and growing to do and still do, but the little girl I used to be would be surprised at what I have endured, experienced, and accomplished thus far. She did not know she had the strength to make it through what I have or to survive and thrive because of it.

Happy Independence Day in Denial

If you think you can get along without other people in your life...you don't like other people...other people get on your nerves...other people are nosy and try to get in your business and tell you what to do...all you need is your laptop or phone and your social media passwords, it is time to come out of denial because we all need other people in our lives. We are social creations and thrive when we work in cooperation with others. We cannot live in a world where we ignore other people and choose not to socialize or interact with others. It doesn't matter what we think about other people. Come out of denial! It is time to take a long, hard look at ourselves and find out why we feel the need to be an island.

I had the idea that being independent and self-sufficient meant not needing other people, but I found out this notion is not true and can be taken too far. Being self-sufficient and managing my responsibilities well is one thing, however, being completely self-reliant and taking care of my responsibilities and myself independently of <u>anyone</u> else is another. Neither definition states that I can be well and live well without interacting with other people. I found out the hard way that I need other people in my life for intellectual stimulation, which can happen through conversations. I need others in my life for support when I am going through challenges and need to talk to someone who understands what I may be experiencing. I need other people to give my love and affection to and receive love and affection in return. I also need to laugh and have fun and share camaraderie with other people. In addition to all of that, I learned how to navigate life by listening and talking with others who have more knowledge, wisdom, and skills than I do. I need to get to the point in my growth that will allow me to be able to converse and interact with people no matter what I really think or feel about them. I'm still working on this, but I am better than I was in my earlier years.

When I was a teenager and young adult in my twenties, I had a fear of some social situations. It was important for me to find out why and how to overcome that fear. I knew I had it, but I denied it for fear of what I would have to endure in order to move through it...even though I knew I would be better for it. I also didn't want other people to know due to ridicule and even more rejection than I already felt.

I attended social events and was very active physically, but I felt most comfortable around close friends and family members. When I did have to go to a non-family social event just prior to and during the height of my depression, I would often become apprehensive and irritable. Many times I would spend the entire time preparing a good excuse not to go. I denied I felt anxiety around social activities, especially after I was diagnosed with depression. During that time, my anxiety was at its pinnacle causing anxiety attacks, which I had never endured before, when there was a social situation ensuing forcing me outside of my comfort zone. This reaction caused me to want to withdraw from people to a greater extent than I had already. However, it was during the height of the depressed state I was in that I realized the importance of good relationships with people and social networks that are supportive, inspiring, and nurturing.

Denial Overload

Right before I decided to see a therapist, I thought I was at my lowest point and wanted to know what was wrong with me. I felt like I couldn't do anything right; I was inferior. My self-esteem was almost non-existent. I was stressed out because I was in college completing my bachelor's. I owned a small studio to train clients. My marital relationship was not meeting my needs. I was in denial about how stressed out I had been until at the end of a training session with a client one day, I realized just how stressed out I was when I started crying. I felt completely exhausted and empty.

I had identified myself with the roles of personal trainer, wife, and student. I didn't know who I was outside of those things. I felt like I had lost a part of me somewhere because I didn't feel like a complete person; I felt fragmented and broken. I kept up a good front though...I tried to anyway. I thought I needed to hide my pain from everyone. Even people I didn't know, but especially from my loved ones. I pretended that everything was ok although I was very angry, sad, and depressed. I thought if I tried to discuss my issues with anyone I would receive ineffectual, unsolicited advice. I felt like I didn't have anyone to talk to about what I was going through because I didn't think I had anyone in my life who really cared enough (this wasn't true), or could give me effective advice, even if they cared. I sought a therapist, a psychologist, whom gave me an impartial shoulder to cry on. All of the things I couldn't tell anyone else because of the judgment that I thought would follow, I could tell her.

What was I trying to avoid? I was trying to avoid pain. I was trying to avoid my fears. I was trying to avoid judgment and confrontation (this seemed at the time an enormous, insurmountable, scary, outlandish fear). Up until that point, I had run from it trying not to look back, but it was always there lurking and lingering in the darkest corners of my psyche waiting for me to be brave enough to walk right up to the door, open it, and walk through—anxiety and all. I couldn't and wouldn't until I knew my current circumstances weren't going to improve; in fact, they seemed to be worsening.

I had to make a decision. Did I want to continue on my current path leading to my slow, but steady destruction or did I want peace, love, and joy?

When we live in denial, it can diminish our enjoyment. It is imperative we give ourselves permission to find out what is holding us back. Doing this leads to steps that transport us out of the shadows into the full saturation of life and its offerings. If you're unable to do that now and you're fearful of taking the steps in route to that point, it is okay. Be patient with yourself. Remember when you want change intensely enough, you will begin to seek what you need to start releasing your denials, setting them free, and sanctioning your truth to ascent to the surface to be lived.

I want you to think for a moment—what would be the first step to lead you in the direction you want to progress? Ask yourself the question and the answer will emerge. You may not want to hear it, but you will get an answer in some way, shape, or form.

Question(s):

- What are you trying to avoid?

- Why are you avoiding?

- How will you move beyond your fears?

- What will your first step be?

Money Hungry: Poem

I don't want to work if I don't have to. I came up with a plan. Living off the kindness of men is where I took my stand. I figured out how to maneuver and be discreet. I learned what I know by watching my brothers play with their women on the street. Now I do the same thing, but I elevated the game. All I have to do is send a text and money falls like rain.

I've got so many men open it doesn't matter if one says no. I'll just pick up another one as I go. It's like shopping at a warehouse; I have privileges so I don't pay. I have a members' platinum card to play. I make sure my skills are intact, keep practicing; gotta be quick on my feet that's what I learned from the street.

Gonna get paid when they want to get laid; gotta pay for rolling in my sheets. I'm eye candy too; can't let my appearance slide. They need to see what they're getting with me. Mother Nature is not on my side. I know I can't do this forever, but for now I'm living the life. So what if I never become a wife. Need more than one, need several, to satisfy my appetite, not for food, or for sex, but for money. Money makes everything all right.

Sure I've had a few who were deranged, a couple that wanted to hit me. I called my boys to take care of them and they did it quickly. Don't know what they did, but it worked out for me. Not gonna let them get the upper hand never waiver from my plan. I'm having too much fun pulling in the next man.

Caught a venereal disease twice before—I got wise and made them all wear a hat. No more dealing with that. I get tested annually want to make sure I'm clean, not spreading anything.

I have one I really like. I know he has a wife, so I trust him to not wear a condom. Gotta show that I trust my boo, that way I get more in the end when he thinks I'm stuck like glue. No not me, can't afford to get stuck. Need at least four to keep up with my desire for more.

It would be nice to just become a wife to a man who is wealthy. A million or more would suffice, but there's no one around like that, where I socialize. I end up with some I don't like. They have enough money to share for a while, so I go out with them and make them smile. They are right for what I need them for. That's all. I want no more.

My bills are all paid. I'm happy. What do I do with the rest? Whatever I want. They don't know that they're dealing with the best. I con them, yes, but I just make it suit me. They do the same; I'm not to blame. I've seen it and had it done to me. I am not gonna give this up until it doesn't work anymore and I can no longer buy them from the store. But for now, I'm milking this cow.

- Angela Taylor

*"Real Knowledge is to know
the extent of one's ignorance."*
- Confucius

Chapter 8

Perks of Denial

Content in My Mess

Sometimes there are parts of our lives we enjoy and don't want to give up in spite of what's going on beneath the surface. So, we deny Truth (our authentic self) when she seeks our attention. These perks and the denials keeping them in place can sometimes keep us from taking steps to beget a more enjoyable life. "We get comfortable in our mess" was the response I overheard from someone. The word mess, as utilized in this book, is defined by Webster as: a situation that is very complicated or difficult to deal with, or a disordered, untidy, offensive, or unpleasant state or condition. My definition is: any thought or series of thoughts that repeats in our minds and causes emotional pain. These thoughts influence everything we experience in our world. They embody the power to destroy relationships (including the one we have with ourselves), careers, progress, future goals, financial increases, etc.

My mess initially felt like a wall I couldn't climb over. Then, it felt as if I was in a prison walking around in circles with every entrance and exit blocked by guards with guns daring me to try to break out. Soon the prison was reduced to a small box within the prison—isolated, dark, damp, and stinky. What benefits do you receive that keep you in your mess, even when you are miserable and hurting inside?

Living The Life

I was comfortable with my lifestyle—I had what I needed and most of what I wanted, but when it came to relationships I seemed disconnected and ended up feeling alienated and rejected. Does this sound like a happy situation? This was a reoccurring theme throughout my life until I finally understood something I already knew intellectually—we are all connected and seeking the same thing, love, even if we don't realize it.

It's not enough to know this intellectually; in order to really understand it I had to begin to apply it to my life and work at it every day. It is something I must continue to work with, like studying and doing homework in school. Completing schoolwork is supposed to help us understand what we are learning, thus, we must practice every day until it becomes an automatic thought like everything else we've learned from our experiencing life.

One of my perks could have been an increase in my finances; after all, I am a skilled person. Any job would have allowed me to buy and do more by utilizing the money I made to stimulate the economy. You have already read about my inappropriate denial interview and years after that experience, I was hired for a position outside of the fitness industry; however, the issues I already had were still there and being pressed down by more issues, I was only there for a short while.

I knew my marital relationship was in trouble, but I ultimately realized all of my relationships (along with my mind, body, and emotions) were in dire need of repair, renewal, and rejuvenation.

Marital Idolatry

In addition to being comfortable with my lifestyle, being married made me feel superior to those women who, in my eyes, couldn't make their marriages work. I didn't know it at the time, but I idolized my marriage. I knew people wanted what they thought we had. I had many people through the years tell me how good we seemed together and they were right. For a while, we were good together, but near the end Truth (the authentic me) kept rearing her beautiful head and I would give her a grimace and slap her face using a denial. *Who is she to tell me what's going on in my life? I'm living it and everything is fine.* After a while I would think, *well, everything isn't fine, but I can fix what isn't working. All I need is a little glue here and there, some plaster to patch up the holes, and a little paint and I'll be fine!* Then Truth would whisper to me (I'm using examples in case some of you out there have heard Truth whisper them in your ear, too), *I don't think we like each other anymore...something has changed...I don't like the way he talks to me...I don't like the way he treats me...I don't like my life...I want to just get in the car and drive and never look back...I'm not supposed to be angry and sad all of the time...Why can't I lose this weight...Why can't I stop eating? What is wrong with me?* Then Deny, using the denials she believes will help me settle down would reply, "We just need a vacation... He's just stressed out about his job and our finances... We have been working too hard and too often for too long...We need a break from everything...We need rest."

On some level was this true? Yes, but this was only on the surface. Going on vacation would have been nice, but we would have taken the issues with us and come back to the same old situation and emotional baggage. The real issues were underneath, kept at bay by Deny.

Being comfortable with my lifestyle and idolizing my marriage kept me there in denial, afraid to face Truth when she showed up with her kind eyes, smiling face, and sparkling white teeth. *I can't lose what I have,* I thought. *We've built this life together. We've been married too long and we've been through too much to just throw it away. If there are couples that have been married for over thirty years and counting, we can do it too!* To this statement Truth said, "You don't know what those couples are going through in order to stay together. You don't know what sacrifices and compromises they've had to make. You're willing to continue living in your box? At what cost? You've lost your joy, your peace, and you don't feel appreciated. Do you want to feel this way for the rest of your life?" Then Deny begins her dialogue, "No, I will not even entertain the thought of separation or divorce…it's not that serious!" All the while, at the height of my depressed state, I felt a knot in my stomach when we were together. I had begun crying every morning and realized later I cried every day for an entire year while trying not to think about, talk about, or do what I knew was inevitable. So after denying, trying, going to therapy, and more denying and trying…I finally came to the realization of what I was trying to avoid—a separation and divorce.

I believe my ex and I are both good people. We are just good people who need different people in our lives.

I believe the relationship served its purpose and ran its course. Yes, we did seek therapy. During that time, I thought maybe we had a chance, but in the subsequent weeks that followed, I realized we each saw completely different futures for ourselves...we had grown apart.

I know some of my readers may not see it so cut and dry because of religious beliefs, cultural traditions, etc., which I respect and I'll add I had my doubts about whether we should stay married until death do us part. However, I came to the realization the relationship died even though we were still alive, well and living in our bodies. I felt like I was dying a slow death physically, mentally, and emotionally. Could an actual physical death be worse than that? I don't think so. I felt like I was in Hell. I had to save what was left of my sanity and myself.

For those of you who may be reading this and thinking, "She's not a Christian!" I will say, "God bless you and I love you in spite of your judgment." The Bible states in John 10:10 that Jesus, when talking to the Pharisees, says, "I am come that they might have life, and have it more abundantly." I count myself as one of the "they" he is speaking about. Jesus did not say he came so his believers could die a slow excruciating death until their bodies finally gave out; he suffered so I wouldn't have to, right?

That relationship wasn't the only one I was in denial about which caused Truth to shake her lovely head at me with the familiar conveyance of love, joy, and peace on her face. She always seemed to look that way. Why was her expression so different from mine? Wasn't what I saw on her face the way I yearned to feel inside and have radiate through me so my face mirrored what my mind and heart felt?

This is just one example of how denial held me captive. I found myself wanting a change, but afraid to take a step forward because of emotions I didn't want to let go of and those I didn't want to feel. Nevertheless, I knew I had to in order for my hands to be open and free to reach for and grab the life I really desired. What are your hands filled with?

Like my marriage, I began to analyze all of my relationships and my role in each, finding myself lacking. During my self-analysis I realized I had given most of my attention, energy, thoughts, effort, emotions, time, days, weeks, months, and years to holding up and maintaining the walls of denial I built to keep myself comfortable... well, uncomfortably comfortable.

All of my relationships were in need of a significant change and it stemmed from me removing, one by one, the denials I used to block Truth from entering my life and spreading her words of love.

Question:

- What are your perks?

Compromise

Compromise can seem like a good idea at the time, but can often lead to dissatisfaction. We sometimes give in to get something we think will be worth the compromise later. Oftentimes, it works out for all concerned and life runs smoother by having done it; that is not what I'm talking about here. There are times when we know we really need or want something, but may think we can live without it because what we're gaining is so much more. We also do things to gain favor, knowing we will pay for it later. I'll give you a few examples: applying to medical school when you know you don't want to be a doctor, but your parents want you to and they're paying your tuition; having some kind of discomfort in your body, but don't consult with a physician; taking on more responsibility when you're already exhausted; saying yes to everything a friend wants you to do because you think saying no would cause them to end the friendship; getting married even though you know the person you are marrying is missing some important qualities; stop attending church services, praying, and/or meditating because you're just too busy; buying a new pair of outrageously expensive designer shoes to impress the women in your circle, knowing you are behind on your rent; marrying someone because they have a lifestyle you want, but you're not in love with the person at all. Those are just a few examples to give you an idea of what I mean by compromise.

When we compromise in these ways, we are listening to Deny. She knows that the compromise seems small and inconsequential in the beginning, but the longer we keep denying our truth, the more severe the collateral damage becomes (see Symptoms of Denial).

As a remedy to the above scenarios, we can hear our Truth whispering: "let your parents know that you would rather become a teacher and get a job to pay for tuition yourself; see a doctor to find out what is really going on in your body; you may want a raise, but with more responsibility comes more stress and strain on your relationships; if saying no means the end of the friendship, that person isn't really your friend; your fiancé may be a wonderful person, but if he/she doesn't have qualities you require in order to remain happy with that person, you will be miserable later and/or seek what you need outside the marriage; you need the inspiration and renewal that comes from weekly and/or daily spiritual nourishment; having a place to reside is a basic need, designer shoes and impressing people are not; being honest is the best way to begin any relationship, especially what is meant to be a lifelong partnership."

When we compromise, it may not feel right. Truth whispers to us that we might want to wait before making a final decision. In another example of a friend wanting us to do something we really do not want to, we push Truth's advice aside and listen to Deny's words comforting us, "Everything will work out. Wouldn't it be selfish to say no to your friend simply because you don't feel like going to the bar tonight? What kind of friend does that make you?" Since you decide to follow Deny's advice, you reluctantly go to the bar. The music is loud (you knew it would be), it's over crowded (it's a Saturday night), there aren't any men you would even want to have a conversation with (just like the last two times you were there), you don't want to drink (you order a Ginger

Ale and orange juice so it looks as if you have a mixed drink), and you sit there watching your friend have the time of her life and making an effort to include you, but you just keep hearing yourself say over and over in your head for hours, *I want to go home. I just want to make a hot cup of Chamomile tea, grab a blanket, sit on my couch, and read a good book.* Is your compromise worth it to you in this moment? No! (If she is a good friend, I could see doing this once in a while, but not often).

We have physical needs (including sexual needs), intellectual needs, emotional needs, and spiritual needs, which must be met in order for our lives to feel authentic to us. If any of these needs are not met, our lives may feel off center. I know my life did; I felt angry and sad more often than usual. I noticed I was getting into arguments more often and had negative thoughts more often. I felt envious or jealous toward people who had what I wanted or were enjoying a lifestyle I wanted to have. I noticed I wanted to be left alone more than I wanted to be around other people and ached to escape from what was going on in my life. I felt exhausted more than usual, yet had extreme emotional highs and lows more often. I wanted to eat sugar infused foods or

208

snack more than usual. I blamed people or situations for the misfortune I perceived I was experiencing.

If you are compromising, you may think about quitting a job, ending a relationship, or you may think about hurting someone. You may be more irritable and curse more often. You may overindulge in food, alcohol, drugs, sex, or other things that become habitual. You may not want to be around happy couples because they remind you of how miserable you really are or how you would want to feel if you had someone you really wanted to be with. You may start to see yourself and others in a negative light. You may begin to think of yourself as better than another group of people. You may not want to be around loved ones because they ask too many questions or give you unsolicited advice and conversely, you may observe people don't want to be around you due to your attitude and/or the drama going on in your life. You may not feel like doing the things that usually bring you joy or at the least make you feel better; you may just have an overall feeling of dissatisfaction about your life in general.

I have noticed all of the above during my tenure with Deny. The above list shows the effects of compromising while living in denial. We get emotional when things are challenging or when they are not going our way, but what I'm suggesting in these situations, we are feeling negative emotions more often and with greater intensity than before the compromising and denying started.

Living a life in denial can often lead to depression because, let's face it, that is what we are doing, pressing the truth down, or suppressing feelings of pain from past trauma, when it wants to come up to the surface. I am including synonyms for depression to help convey my point. You might feel dejected, sad, melancholy, despair, hopeless, pessimistic, despondent, gloomy, discouraged, downhearted, or sluggish.

Some synonyms for repression are the actions we take when we compromise while in denial about something in our lives, we often: censor ourselves or others, suppress, quash our truth, control, bound thoughts and emotions that want to be expressed, and constrain. Suppression synonyms are: crush, restrain, interdict, check, curb, arrest, repress, deter, inhibit, and block (ABC Thesaurus.com).

Question(s):

- Do you feel as if you are trying to hold something back, keep it in, or down and away from your conscious thoughts?

- What are you suppressing?

- What have you compromised for the sake of the greater good that may be doing more harm to you than good?

Defend 'til the End: Poem

That is not why I said it.
That is not what I meant.
That is not why I did it.
I just forgot about it.
I did not intend to say that.
I did not say that to offend you.
I did not intend to do that.
That was a mistake, what I meant to do...
I was just kidding, joking, and having fun.
That was a Freudian slip,
A slip of the tongue.
I am not sensitive around that subject.
I do not get defensive. You misjudged it...
I'm not temperamental, touchy, or testy.
I'm getting fed up with your accusations, don't you see?
I'm not raising my voice! I just talk loud!
You're misunderstanding me. I'm not proud.
I am listening. You're not making any sense.
Please someone make them understand.
Help with my defense.

- Angela Taylor

"Turn your wounds into wisdom."

- Oprah Winfrey

Chapter 9

Signs and Symptoms of Denial

As Deny creates chaos in our minds causing it to work overtime, our cognitive abilities and physical bodies can begin to break down under the pressure and display signs and symptoms as a result of the chaos she instigates. Living in denial led to an increase of stress, anxiety attacks, and depression for me.

As I have stated earlier, more often than not, we tend to exclude the mental and emotional parts of ourselves from the health, wellness, and healing conversations. Instead, we think of ourselves as disconnected parts and pieces, entities fragmented and isolated from one another, when we are whole beings with each part of us working in unison. Everything that affects your mind affects your body and vice versa. Do you think of your mind and emotions when you think of your health or only your body? I challenge you to begin to think of yourself as a whole integrated system.

Think about what happens when a virus invades your computer and begins to rewrite code, multiply itself, and corrupt your programs. If not stopped, it will eventually crash your whole computer. Viruses multiply and spread; they don't tell each other to stay in one small-contained area—wherever they can go, they will. Think of denials in that way. They influence your thoughts, attitudes, and behavior. In turn, your body responds immediately to the thoughts and emotions you entertain. For example, you may feel anxious or stressed and experience an increase in heart rate. You may feel a headache coming on, which will affect your mood and motivation. In turn, your lack of motivation affects your attitudes and behaviors. Soon your whole system is compromised and before you know it you're crashing…

areas of your life affected by the denials continue to regress until you're flat on your back wondering what happened. It could be as simple as a minor headache that develops into a migraine.

Here is my list of some of the signs and symptoms I endured because of denial. I will give you my list first and then you compare it with yours. How many items on your list coincide with mine?

I was in denial about what I thought and how I felt about situations, people in my life, and myself. When I began exhibiting physical ailments, it was easy for me to deny they had anything to do with my mental and emotional state. After my list of signs and symptoms, I have included a few journal entries so that you can read exactly what I wrote in my journals during the time I was experiencing signs and symptoms of stress due to the stories of denials I lived.

Poems will follow that are appropriate for and organized into the "Eight Areas of the Circle of Life." The list is as follows: Body, Mental, Emotional, Relationships, Finances, Career/Lifestyle, Energy, and Spiritual.

Journal Entries

Tuesday, April 8, 2008, 6:59 p.m.

I've just discovered that it's my nerves making my hair break off. I've noticed an increase in breakage over the last couple of weeks and now I see the result of it. My hair on the left side is thinner than on the right and there's a patch on the side (right) that's very short. I can't blame it on the braids or the perm because I haven't had either one. I NEED TO RELAX MORE!!!

I had to lead the Exercise Programming class in a discussion today and I purposely relaxed my mind and gave it to God. I don't usually notice when I'm stressed, but lately I have noticed an increase in breakage when I combed my hair. I would end up with a ball of hair in the sink and wonder why. I would dismiss it and say, "Oh, my hair is just shedding," but it wasn't. I've also been very tired lately. I slept four hours yesterday afternoon. I've slept two hours this afternoon. Sometimes I just get to the point where I have to lie down and can't go any further. That's how I was yesterday.

I've been making an effort to eat fewer calories during the day to promote weight loss. Sometimes, especially on weekends, I eat more and justify it by telling myself that I was good all week.

I exercised yesterday, too. I rode the SPINNING bike for forty minutes and then finished out the hour on the treadmill. I pushed myself, but not too hard. That may have contributed to my tiredness, too. I have been feeling stiff and tight and really needed to exercise and stretch. I haven't done any of that today.

Larry's been feeling tired too and wondering why. I think it's because he won't get the rest he needs when he can, so he has days when he just can't get going. Last weekend was one of them.

I'm taking the "Lessons in Truth" class at church. We have another week or two of classes. I did well on the exam. I earned one hundred percent. That's extra work too, but I wanted to complete it so that I can get more involved in church activities and refresh my memory. I want to get out of my own way and let Spirit guide me. That's why I've been so wound up. I'm trying to do everything on my own and not lean on God enough, not releasing things into God's care and keeping.

I haven't been meditating lately and I need to do that. I'm going to eat a little something now before it gets too late.

April 9, 2008, 5:03 p.m.

I went to the doctor today. He told me to buy some Musinex for my sinuses. He said there was no enlargement of my nodes and everything looked fine physically. I had blood taken and gave a urine sample. He told me to call next week Tuesday to get the results and ask the nurse to mail me a copy of the results. I told him how tired I've been. He asked me if I was depressed. I told him I didn't feel depressed. We'll see what the results are from the blood work and urine sample. If it isn't physical, it has to be mental, emotional, or spiritual.

It's probably more mental and emotional than anything. School is challenging. I'm trying to maintain good grades and learn as much as I can and also work on being more open to people. In the three years of being there I haven't really made any friends because I don't talk with anyone. I feel unsure of myself, not confident sometimes. Why am I not secure in my own skin? Why do I feel the need to hide? I'm also dealing with thoughts of my weight and how I should look like a personal trainer, but I don't think I do at the moment. It's not as easy as I thought it was going to be to get the weight off. It doesn't seem to be budging at all. Although I feel smaller and look a bit smaller when I look in the mirror. I'm making an effort to eat smaller meals, but sometimes at some meals I eat more and then feel bad because I didn't stick to my nutritious meals or ate too much or consumed too many calories.

With all of this going on, how could I possibly feel relaxed and at peace. I'm a trainer and I feel like a failure at what I'm training others to do and be. Does my need to win drain me of power?

My Signs and Symptoms

Results of my denials that led to stress, weight gain, anxiety, and, ultimately, a depression diagnosis.

- Hair breakage
- Eating larger meals
- Eating more often
- Eating more sugar
- Weight gain
- Stopped exercising
- Started exercising
- Stopped exercising
- Started walking
- Started weight training
- Working from sun up to sun down
- Resistance low/caught a cold
- Stopped exercising
- Ate less
- Got better
- Ate more
- Mood swings
- More hair breakage
- Pre-menstrual Syndrome (PMS) worse
- Night sweats, onset of PMS more often
- Feeling angry, sustained longer periods of time.
- Feeling angry, increased intensity
- Ate more chocolate
- Ate larger meals
- Ate more sugar
- Ate more processed food
- Ate less home cooked meals

- Drinking more soda
- Skin irritation, chronic
- Apprehension started, chronic
- Pneumonia
- Hair breakage, periodically
- Developed a chronic cough
- Acid reflux diagnosis
- Anxiety, chronic
- Nervousness, chronic
- Sadness, chronic
- Feeling confused about my life
- Wanting to withdraw more from people
- Calling people less
- Feeling a knot in stomach
- Feeling abandoned emotionally
- Hair breakage, continues
- Migraine headaches during PMS, chronic
- Anxiety before bed/heart racing
- Stress high, chronic
- Feel adrenalin surges during sleep, chronic
- Contracted shingles
- Insomnia, chronic
- Exhaustion, chronic
- Up in the middle of the night, chronic
- Snacking all the time
- Sadness upon rising
- Not looking forward to a new day, chronic
- Nightmares, chronic
- Crying, chronic
- Deep sadness, chronic
- Upset stomach, chronic

- Anxiety attacks during the day
- Sleeping excessively
- Weight gain
- Too exhausted to exercise
- Loss of motivation
- Feelings of despair
- Disinterest in normal activities and responsibilities
- Uninspired

The 8 Areas of the Circle of Life

Signs and Symptoms: Poems

Body

Stuck in The Middle: Poem

It does not seem to want to cooperate.

And do what I want it to do.

In and out, up and down it goes.

My mind does not seem to control it.

It has a mind of its own.

I know what to do. It has been effective for years,

But now, what I do doesn't seem to change anything.

Reps and sets, miles and minutes,

Free weights and machines,

Inside, outside, topside, bottom,

It does not seem to matter which.

Flats and hills, walking and cycling,
Stairs, jump rope, track, field, paved and dirt trails,
Bells, balls, boards, bands, bars, bags, brackets,
Cones, ladders, hoops. I have it all.
Even bottles of water and towels
To soak up the sweat that pours,
But when all is done, without speaking a word,
The scale shows the same numbers or adds a few.
Could it be muscle mass?
Hypertrophy would be welcomed.
Yes, some I would imagine, but most, I doubt.
When I look in the mirror I want to see less
Of what was there yesterday,
Less of me...what has become more of me.
Front, back, top, and bottom, smooth and sculpted,
Not too much, just enough to show that I work.
Maybe I should put down this chocolate bar,
Get out of this chair
And stop daydreaming,
But my favorite show is coming on
I'll start again tomorrow.

- Angela Taylor

Mental

My To-Dos: Poem

I am on a roll. Life is good. Busy as a bee,
But it pleases me.
No time for foolishness. No mess,
Just impress my mind with my to-do list.
Filling up nicely, the way I like to see.
Checking off my to-do is thrilling.
To see the work I have completed always willing
To go the extra mile. Not often with a smile,
But getting things done one by one.
By the wayside, some things fall.
I'll catch up to them later
Gotta keep them in a separate directory
And file them under a different category.
Someday someone will tell my story
And it will be loaded with accomplishments.
Those were first on my list, unseen to everyone but me,
Then out in the open where I want them to be.
Yes, my to-do list is full. It shows I mean business
No loitering today or tomorrow.

No time to feel any sorrow
Trying to seep up through the crevices
Too narrow to be filled by much at one time
Just a letter or two that become words
That sometimes rhyme,
Telling me to, "Slow down. Take it easy.
Patience is a virtue.
No need to rush here and there,
Feeling as if you are getting nowhere
Sit and listen awhile.
What you hear may make you smile."
But I say I have no time to sit and smile,
Too much around here to complete.
If you knew the half of it,
You wouldn't be telling me to take a seat.
Time is passing. It waits for no one.
Gotta get what is mine. Can't wait on time.
Won't be here for very long. Once I'm gone
I'll have some things to show I have been here.
Working to complete my assignments.
Checking off my to-do lists.
One in every room of my house,
Even the drawers are filled with them.
Past and future listings,
Recordings of my intentions, grand schemes,
And some I dare not mention,
Private to-do's registered in secret places.
Known only to one other.
He will appreciate my catalog.
Will rank it high on a scale from one to ten
And want to do my list again and again.

My life is abundant with directories—
Goals, aspirations, desires, dreams,
Plans to take me where I want to go
Step-by-step, one stage to the next.
Up the ladder and onto the next platform
Up, up I go.
Never looking back at what's been missed
But it reveals itself to me from the cracks
Seeps in one letter at a time
Forming sentences, paragraphs, and stories
Reminding me of my to-do's
Left from weeks ago when I started a new list
Seeking another destination.
On and on and around I go,
Where will my to-do lists stop? They won't.
I'll be looking at a to-do list when my time is up
From climbing the ladder, purpose to purpose,
Graduating with each check mark.
The same way I began, is the way I will end.

- Angela Taylor

Emotional

Exhausted: Poem

A shriveled up raisin fallen by the curb
In the early morning
From a raisin box someone dropped as the sun rose
The air sucked out of me—
No vitality, exhausted
Physically, mentally, and emotionally.
Fatigue overflows from my brain cells
And leaks into every crevice and orifice
Of my body. My organs are filled with it—
No thoughts, no words, no memory.
Do not ask me to do anything;
I am straining just to stay alive,
Weary from my journey;
After falling to the ground
Speckles of dirt in my folds
No one will want me now.
I have gotten lost from the rest

A vagabond on my own without a friend in sight
Worn out from toiling down here
Trying to find my way back home, lost
In this massive pile people walk on
Never hearing my cries as I look for some sign
That I will be ok
That I will eventually find my way
But for now alone, scared, and confused
Which way is home? I don't know.
I'll just stay here. Can't roll another inch
Worn from my tour of the soil. Lost in the dust,
No energy left to toil.

- Angela Taylor

Relationships

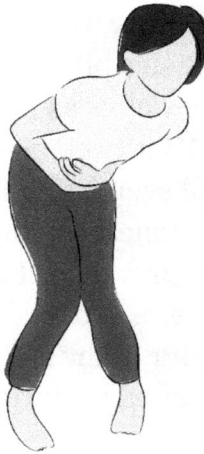

Pangs of Truth: Poem

She cooks breakfast for the two of them and they both sit down to eat. He doesn't even look at her. She feels uneasy and readjusts in her seat. They eat in silence and his head is down, but he appears to be in deep thought. He's not sharing any thoughts with her so she just sits there waiting for him to spit it out.

She sits and she waits, but nothing is said. She doesn't know what subject to bring up.

He hasn't been interested in discussing anything with her lately. He seems to have just given up. Everything she thinks of she knows is of no interest to him, so she just eats her food while looking around the kitchen. When she looks at him, his eyes are cast down so she continues this way for a while. But as she chews her food, the knot in her stomach grows larger until it feels like a softball stuck in her gut; she rubs her stomach and leans forward feeling as if she's going to chuck. He doesn't say a word just keeps eating his food as if he's sitting there alone. Why do we have meals together if we don't have anything to say? I should just go get on the phone.

We may as well eat in separate rooms—that would be better for me anyway. I don't understand why he's not interested in my day, what I'm involved in or what my future plans might be. I'm interested in him and all that he has to say when he talks about his day to me.

Do I just not interest him anymore? Is he angry, or hurt, what? Every time I ask him what's wrong he just says nothing and continues with his thoughts.

Maybe he just doesn't like me anymore. He's grown tired of me over the years. Her stomach begins to cramp as she holds back her tears.

"I think I feel sick," she says, as she stands up and runs from the table. The bathroom is close so she gets to the toilet quickly. She throws up her food until there's no more left, until she no longer feels sickly. She doesn't understand why; this is the third time this week. She knows she's not pregnant. Let's see what else it could be. The food was fresh and he's not sick, so let me sit and get clear.

She rinses her mouth and brushes her teeth before swishing the mouthwash around then looks at her face, pale as a sheet, sits down on the tub with her face in her hands as she looks down towards the ground. I'm tired of feeling this way. Something is wrong.

He doesn't care anymore, hasn't even seemed to notice I'm gone. I don't like how this feels. I can't go on this way. We both have nothing to say.

What is this knot in my stomach telling me that I don't already know anyway? But what can I do about the situation? I don't have a job; I can't just go. My mind has told me time and time again to save up my money not to spend it all on food, but my mind is so damn confused right now it's the food that keeps me in a decent mood.

She goes back to the kitchen and sits back in her seat. He asks if she's ok and just continues to eat. Then he gets up from the table, leaves his plate sitting there, walks to the bathroom to wash his hands, and walks to the family room to sit in his chair. *Guess I'll be eating the rest of my meal alone*, she says to herself with a groan. She shakes her head, picks up her fork, and sits there, the knot back in her stomach, Truth trying to get her attention. I don't like him anymore and he doesn't seem to care for me. What are we doing here? We were a family. She pushes the food around on her plate for a few seconds, gets up, scrapes the scraps in the trash, looks at his plate and walks away. She washes her hands, dries them, and stands in the bathroom trying to decide which way to go. She walks to the family room, sits in the chair beside him, looks at the TV screen, and asks him, "What's on?"

- Angela Taylor

Finances

Where Is My Money: Poem

The affirmations aren't working.

Has God been listening?

I have gone to church every Sunday

Has God been watching?

I closed my eyes and prayed after

I wrote the check for my tithes

And put my last dollar in the offering this morning.

Did God notice?

In the Bible a woman gave all she had

And she was blessed with more;

I know His word!

I gave the change from my car to the bag lady

who stands in the street holding a sign—

That was my good deed.

Where is my money?

When is it coming?

I don't see it anywhere.

Come on God, I know that you know I need it

I didn't go to the boat last week.

I didn't put that diamond I wanted on my card...

This time.

I didn't even go out with my friends Friday.

I have sacrificed a lot!

When is my money going to get here?

I need it right now!

What else do I need to do to get your attention?

Shout?

I know You work in quietness,

But my mind is too cluttered

Worrying about my money drought.

God, why are you holding onto my blessing?

Where are you, somewhere resting?

- Angela Taylor

Career and Lifestyle

The Scion 1: Poem

The two of them together created me;
Together no more. He left. She carried me,
Deflated and blue,
Kept me fed on good home cooking,
But I starved just the same
Others stepped in, molded me, scolded me,
Showed me what to do,
How to act, what to say, who to be.
They were the directors of my story
Characterized and brought to life by me.
Not my fault, not responsible, it was them.
They are to blame.
Had no choice but to live what I learned...from them.
Now they look at me in disbelief.
Can't believe the things I've done.
He wouldn't do that, mom says
When told of my latest circumstance.
She knows me,
But chooses to see what her imagination tells her I be.

Not my fault. They made me this way. All of them.
Now they have to live with what they've done,
Think about it every time my name is mentioned
Shake their heads and point their fingers,
But they know I was molded by their vision of who
They thought I would be.
A curse, good for nothing, just like my father they said.
No shame. I'm not to blame,
They are responsible for who I've become.
I am not a slice of my momma's sweet potato pie,
Sliced and divided from the whole
Because I look good to eat.
I'm just a crumb, attached to nothing
And shaking in the center of the pan
Filled with the same ingredients,
But still empty like the container it sits in.
There is nowhere for me to hide. I was left behind
By the others who were lucky enough
To stay close to the crumbs undivided and unified,
Picked up as a whole slice, chosen.
The crumb is left to fend for itself with no one to care
It is even there, lost in the container it was baked in.

-Angela Taylor

The Scion 2: Poem

Another side of the coin--
The two of them together created me. Still together.
Whatever, I don't really care.
I get what I need when I shake the money tree.
I get what I want, no responsibility;
That's for poor kids. I'm in a different bracket,
On my own most of the time, they don't know what I do.
They both work almost non-stop.
Get what you want. Is what I hear most.
I have privilege, girls in abundance.
Parties every weekend. I'm always invited.
They know I get it started.
I'm live and wired.
Big stash in my car hidden from view.
Last time cops threw it out. Got in trouble.
Now gotta make double to cover what I lost.
No mind, next party will set me up straight.
Business is right. They made it that way.
What I don't earn I get from my parents,
So I don't have to wait to save up my pennies,
More like hundreds for me,
Spending on whatever I want. No responsibility.
They don't know what I do.
They don't seem to have a clue.

Think my bling is expensive,
Yet they don't ask questions,
Just wave goodbye, out the door. Work to do.
Call after school so we know you're safe.
"I will," I say. "Have a nice day!"
"Sir, your son is at the station, picked up for possession.
Come get him. He's being released with a warning.
He's a kid deserves a break,
Doesn't understand what he's doing,
That he's making a mistake.
He's just a boy. Give him a talk and he'll be fine,
No problem, doesn't have to do time."
On the street once again. No responsibility.
Taken care of. Boy am I lucky to have parents
Who love me enough to save me from myself.
Another day at school, invited to the next party.
I go to the car to check my stash, all set.
I'm just a boy, I make mistakes,
But I have a helping hand.
My dad has friends around this town,
So I can continue with my plans.
Not my fault they work so much.
They created the situation.
I'm just making the most of it, what else can I do?
I'm a product, their creation.
My life is what they've made it. No judgment calls to
make.
Thanks mom and dad!
My life is great!

- Angela Taylor

Energy

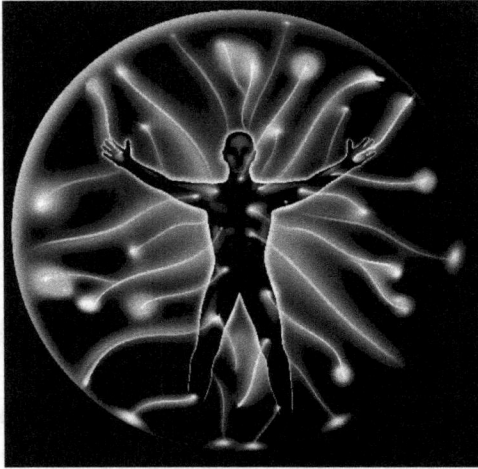

The Energy that I Am: Poem

I close my eyes and I can feel it.
The smile on my face may give it away.
There are a few things that may come close,
However, may not last as long.
I can drift forever enjoying the reverberations of elation.
I can stay in this moment,
Aware each instant of the tingling of electricity—
Dynamic, my cells, atoms, and the subs.
I am starlight dispersed inside a nebula.
I feel as if I am radiating vitality.
It pulsates through my heart and with each breath
Floods my capillaries with the nourishment it requires,
But seldom receives because I get too busy
To recognize the hunger and thirst of my cells delight.
It feels so good, I want to keep surfing this wave of bliss.

It transforms my mood, my thoughts stop.
I am in it, connected to it, surging and merging with it,
I AM IT.
Content and complete in this space.
Everything else is secondary
To this fire that can only be perceived
By the smile on my face.

Kinetic energy swirling in the atmosphere of earth
Dancing with the vibrancy of color and sound emanating
From everything
Mixing... creating a painting of perfectly
Blended and vivid hues.
Minute streaks on the canvas of the universe
Glowing brightly for all to see,
If only by the smile on my face.

- Angela Taylor

Spiritual

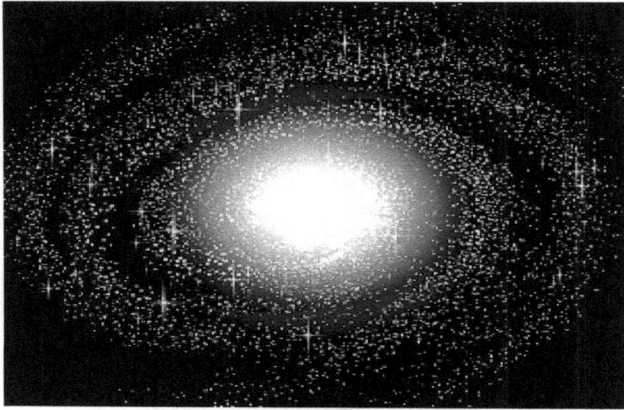

I AM: Poem

Creator and creation
Energy Universal
Phenomenon and Noumenon
Consciousness
Incomprehensible to the human psyche.

I AM the quantum field, moons, planets,
And stars in every form.
I AM compressed light
And dispersed darkness, deep and vast.
I cool and fall, then heat and rise exploding with
Unimaginable force in a shower of radiance.
I evolve from infancy to full maturation illuminating
Majesty in all of my glory.

They say as a star in death I AM a white dwarf,
But my core is still alive with energy
Even after I have propelled myself into vastness
To create new life beyond the appearance.

I AM EVERLASTING.

I AM the Milky Way Galaxy and the billions of galaxies
Beyond this spec, a mere stitch in my fabric
That as an individual I call home.
I AM a singularity so powerful nothing escapes me.
I AM dark matter, white matter,
Subatomic particles that comprise
Hydrogen, helium atoms, and the void.
I AM ethereal... Life,
Manifesting for 13.7 billion years and counting.

Through the illusion of the interpretation of the mind,
I AM viewed through a lens of restriction,
Impeded by skewed perceptions
In which mortality fights and dies to perpetuate
Its belief in limitations.

I AM GRANDIOSE
And also minute,
Dangling from the peak of a concept.

- Angela Taylor

A Perfect Union: Poem

I am an elegant individual
As proclaimed by science...in design.
My essence embraces all.
I am a slice selected from the whole sweet potato pie,
Yet every ingredient added to the whole,
Is also here inside my crust, golden brown...my skin.
Like the sweet potatoes, butter, and brown sugar
That comprise the pie, I contain systems,
Formed particles of energy created
From the moment of conception
To clothe, protect, support, sustain, repair,
And re-energize.

I am aware of everything.
Connected by consciousness
That is sensation and inspiration
Housed in one intricately complex package.
I know the secrets of life.
I hear them reverberate with every pulse.
They collide, mix and mingle with the hemoglobin
In my blood. They intertwine with the lymph
As it collects the debris left behind by lies.
I AM here and there right now.
My vitality can be seen, touched, heard, smelled,
And tasted, yet never experienced.
I talk frequently, but I AM rarely listened to.
I AM variety, the spice of life.
My true flavor is beyond comprehension.
Humanity can only withstand a sample of Me,
And that they savor...infinitely.
I AM visible, yet unseen...
The space in between is a mystery to most.
They overlook that part of what I AM to view what is real
to them, **my humanity,**
Using the instrument of choice—a blind eye.

- Angela Taylor

Question(s):

- What are your signs and symptoms of stress or denial in each area of the circle of life?

A Mother's Love: Poem

She is my baby.

A beauty second to none.

Talent beyond compare.

The smartest in her class.

Everybody loves her.

A kind word for everyone.

She is a good mother to her children.

All that a mother could ask for.

She's my only, you know.

Took care of her as best I could.

Loves me too, tells me so.

Down on her luck a few times too many.

Had to do what she had to, is what she told me.

I know what it's like; I've been down on my luck
A time or two.
Wasn't always saved.
I did what I needed to do when
Money was tight and the rent was due and
I had to feed her, too.
I believe she's doing her best.
She is just like me when I was her age.
She's a good girl. They don't know her like I do.
When she is doing her best, what else can she do?
She'll always be my baby. No matter what they say.
I don't listen to any of them anyway.

- Angela Taylor

"If you can't forgive and forget, pick one."

- Robert Brault

Chapter 10

My Chamber of Denials

When I chose the path that would lead to peace, love, and joy, what I was afraid of (my denial stories and reasons behind them) became secondary. What I wanted to experience became my primary focus. I had to be brave and tell myself that no matter what I had to go through in order to achieve what I wanted, I would. I still saw them as obstacles, but obstacles I could and would move through in order to gain the life I really wanted.

The first step leading to my new life was examining my current life and determining why I started having anxiety attacks and crying every morning. This was when I detected the denial stories I had been pushing away from my conscious mind in order to maintain the appearance of contentment. After I acknowledged the denials, I had to figure out what I could do to change my situation so that I could begin to feel my joy again. At that time, I didn't have anyone around whom I thought could give me objective advice and counsel, so I decided to seek a mental health professional.

Know Your Truth

The next step was to work therapy to my benefit. I needed to talk about everything locked inside of me since childhood. I talked and talked. I spoke about the circumstances I was born into, my immediate family, and the relationships between us. I confessed what I thought my mom and dad's issues were and how I felt like I was in the middle of their mess when I was a child as well as what I perceived my parents' individual personal issues were, independent of their relationship.

I talked about my marital relationships and issues. Of course I talked about each of us and my perception of how I thought this affected the condition of our relationship and me. Additionally, I expressed my thoughts, feelings, and perceptions about all of the people in my life, including myself. Once I released all the tension that was building deep within my chest, I felt better.

Next was the analyzation of my circumstances and narrowing everything down to my relationships before ultimately arriving at myself. I understood that the relationships between the people around me in my immediate environment as a child affected me in many ways that I resented, but, as an adult, I came to comprehend I had to let it all go. I analyzed each relationship and began receiving inspiration about how to make each one better. It all started with me changing my attitude and behavior by changing my perceptions about the people, the relationships I had with them, and my role in each.

I examined each relationship and let the thoughts and emotions about each one come to my conscious awareness. As I felt the emotions and thoughts about the conversations I had with them and the behavior of the people involved, I began to reflect about my role in the relationships. I thought about my attitude toward them and the reasons for my attitude; also my issues that may have led to some of the decisions I made, things I said, and actions I took that either made the relationship better or worse. I had to own up to my issues and understand the kind of person I was having a relationship with. This forced me to decide whether or not I wanted to continue with the relationship.

It was important for me to be honest about the relationship, weighing the pros and cons, examining my fears and perks, and enact a difficult decision in some cases; however, one that would be beneficial for all concerned moving forward.

I began to see these people I interacted with as people and not adversaries who inflicted pain and torture just because they could. I had to see them as human beings with their own ideas, perceptions, fears, joys, sorrows, challenges, problems, issues, habits, circumstances, coping mechanisms, and denial stories that they dealt with every day, which had nothing to do with me.

Once I began to see them as just people, I asked myself some challenging questions. I knew the answers were going to be a challenge to deal with if the relationship didn't have a good prognosis. I asked myself: *Is this a relationship supportive of me being healthy, strong, and vital, or is it a relationship detaining me in denial and hiding from the truth? Does this relationship benefit me in any way, and if so, how? Can I be my authentic self without feeling guilty or bad in some way? Do I feel good around this person or group of people? Am I growing and learning anything that is nourishing and edifying to my mind?*

If I didn't find the person or group of people to be a positive influence or an asset of my new life and me, I ended the relationship or limited my communication with him/her/them. This had to happen even though the people in my life were good people—just not the right people I need in my life right now. I felt guilty about this at first, but I had to think of it as self-preservation. Just because they're good people, doesn't mean they have to stay in my life if they are not <u>good for me or good to me.</u>

We receive benefits from being in relationships we don't want to give up, but we need to weigh the pros and cons. If the cons outweigh the pros, it's time to say goodbye. If you have challenges with confrontation like I did (...do...did?), when you begin to focus on what you want in life, as opposed to what you don't, it may be easier for you to confront this challenge. If not, you can simply cease calling or taking their calls or visiting them. They'll get the message eventually. Is that passive aggressive? Yes, but I understand that pain, so I'll give you an out.

It's important to seek help when needed. It doesn't matter what other people think about with whom we seek help from. What matters is retrieving the help in order to feel better and live the life we want.

It's imperative to remember YOU are important. Like they say, "If you die before the people you put first, who will take care of them when you're gone?" Who will love your baby and give him/her the nurturing necessary when you're gone? Who will love your children and make sure they're safe when you're gone? Who will make love to your significant other and be his or her rock after you are buried, simply because you failed to make sure you are well and operating at optimal capacity?

Remember, our mind and emotions are connected to our bodies. Who will take care of them if we don't? It's our responsibility and no one else's. When Deny tries to tell you it is someone else's responsibility to make sure you stay well, let your truth be your guide and lead you into victory, while Deny finds another victim to lovingly torture.

Parents

I had to see my parents as people and realize they had their own set of issues as individuals and as a couple. I had to realize they did the best they knew how with what they were given, even with all of the denials they were living. It is hard to teach your children something you haven't learned yourself. In fact, it is impossible. I had to understand that although I wished my relationship with each of them, and between us all, could have been different, they were what they were. As an adult, it was important for me to understand that no matter how hard I wished, hoped, and prayed things had been different, I had to accept the way they were and forgive. When I decided to forgive, I became more empathetic instead of judgmental toward my parents. I know they did the best they could with what they had to offer. They had their own issues influenced by their upbringing, experiences, knowledge, wisdom, emotional maturity, etc. They are imperfect beings just like me, and made it the best way they knew how, just like the rest of us and for that I love them. Our parents are not gods and goddesses who know it all. They are humans who learn as they go; understanding that was significant and a real epiphany for me. By changing my perception of them, I could forgive them. I could put myself in their place and understand whatever was said or done was not done out of spite, but out of their humanity…fallible and flawed, but human. I had to realize I am not my parents and they are not me. When I say flawed I mean we all make mistakes. We all say things we don't really mean when we are frustrated or angry. We all have our own perceptions of what we encounter that causes us to behave in ways we may not want or even understand. I got it, finally.

After being angry for decades about things that were said and done that I thought shouldn't have been, I was able to release it all. I realized I am not perfect myself, so how can I judge them for not being perfect or meeting my expectations as parents. They are who they are; I could either accept that fact and move on to enjoy my life in peace, or continue to be angry and hurt, blaming them for something they may have been completely unaware of. They were trying to figure out how to navigate their own issues while raising us. I experienced Deny wreaking havoc in their lives and my siblings and I were caught in the middle.

The assistance I needed came from my environment (therapy) and from within. I had to let my Truth speak and listen with an open heart and mind knowing that what I desired from my relationships and myself was absolutely possible. I only needed to realize that and act on it without letting my fears stop me from imagining more, expecting more and reaching for what I knew was waiting for me to become aware was possible to have.

Question(s):
- What is the truth about how you interact with others?

- What issues are keeping you from having more harmonious relationships?

- Which relationships need a closer examination to determine its maintenance in your life?

- Have you forgiven the people in your life, especially your parents for being human and making mistakes?

- With whom or what circumstances are you having a difficult time forgiving in your life? Ask yourself why and let your truth speak.

Healing in Hell: Poem

Scorched beyond recognition,
Burned by the heat from the images I hold
Plastic surgery can't undo what I have done...
What I have created and encouraged to
Permeate, grow, and expand,
Now feeling trapped in hell—the hell I made for myself.
As cool and refreshing as a tall glass of ice water,
My life looks normal viewed from outside,
Yet it feels more like I'm an ant dancing on top of a log
inside of a fireplace.
I designed this room, bought the furnishings,
Painted the walls,
Fluffed the pillows and folded the towels.
My place just the way I wanted it, but wait—
Where did all of this heat come from?
Denial, confusion, frustration, resignation,
All from me. Nobody else is at fault.

I chose the king-size bed
With the pillow top sitting in the corner
Away from the windows
Where the curtains I chose are draped.
All of my choices are around me,
The result of the decisions I made
Using antiquated memories
Deteriorating from years of reliving the same stories
Until I made a different choice.
I chose to look ahead instead of behind;
I chose to bring my present and future
Out of obscurity and back in view,
But they both got lost
In the shuffle of my everyday activities.
I want Love, Joy, Peace, and Harmony
To saturate my thoughts, quench the fire
And repair my life like nothing else can.
As I plan for the possibilities that lie ahead,
These are the qualities I want to feel consistently,
Anticipating action, and adventure around every corner,
The inside of my glass matching the outside.
I'm an ant floating on a leaf in a pond
Square dancing with a ladybug
No longer in hell, but Heaven,
Spelled **M-Y L-I-F-E**

- Angela Taylor

"Man is not the creature of circumstances.
Circumstances are the creatures of men."
- Benjamin Disraeli

Chapter 11

Release

It was important to understand that those who I thought harmed me in some way were marvelous, imperfect human beings (just like me) making it through life the best way they knew how and if they knew a better way of being, they would have done better. I also had to understand that I had to take responsibility for my skewed perceptions, which affects my attitudes and shapes my behavior. I had to realize I had issues that needed to be worked out and therefore could not blame the other individuals solely for the condition of our relationships.

Investigation of My Hell

When I finally understood this, I had to stop running from myself and deal with the issues I knew were there. I sat myself down and had a heart-to-heart with the little girl, the teenager, and the young adult Angela. We talked on and on for minutes at a time, sometimes for hours at a time and many days. My girls had a lot to talk about. I listened intently and began to understand the inner workings of my own psyche. I realized things that I knew, but had suppressed and the suppression of this information caused me to behave in certain ways that served to protect me at that time, but ceased to serve me in my present and was detrimental to my future happiness. I had to face the fact there were things about me I did not like and needed to change if I wanted to see the results in my life I desired.

My girls told me about their doubts and fears. We cried together...a lot. I began to feel the loosening of the knots that had my muscles taut from the stress I carried around all of these years. I remember often when I visited a Napropath for the first time and after examining me he said, "You are too young (I was sixteen) to be so tense. I knew that I always felt like a fawn encircled by hungry, drooling lions licking their chops because I was dinner, for at least one of them. I didn't realize it was affecting my body. After conversing with my former selves and releasing the pinned up negative emotional energy (see chapter 12), I felt a release from all of the tension I had been holding inside of me since I was a child. It felt good...better than good. It felt fantastic.

It was a challenge listening to what I had to say because I did not want to hear these things and had pushed them away because of the inadequacy I felt while thinking about what I saw as my shortcomings. It's hard to hear the truth about yourself even when it is coming from you, hence, the denial.

As I got reacquainted with myself from all of my stages of life, I felt whole. I felt like I understood me. It felt good to understand why I did what I did and interacted the way I did with people while trying to understand myself at the same time. I knew that I still needed to work on these challenges, however, it just felt good to know there was a reason behind it all and with my newfound insight, I could begin to reconnect the split between my heart (emotions) and my mind (intellect).

Journal Entry

December 2013

I've been feeling so frustrated lately. I want so much more out of life and myself than I'm experiencing right now. What's stopping me from experiencing the joy of life? What's stopping me from being who I want to be instead of living and feeling like I'm only existing, being only a one dimensional caricature of what I have settled for? Why have I settled? Why do I feel stuck between where I am now and where I want to be? My beliefs about who I am and what I am able to accomplish based on what I've experienced in my past. The beliefs I have about the way I should live life as a wife; believing that I should make myself small for the sake of a union that may or may not be the one I should continue to stay in.

I feel as if I've made myself small. I feel like I'm in a cage, although of course physically I'm not. I often wonder what it is holding me back from venturing out and being the person I really am, fully. Why do I feel so dissatisfied with my life? The relationship I'm in is not what I dreamed it would be. I feel as if somewhere along the line we lost our friendship. We no longer have that light and playful feeling we once had. Everything seems so dark and serious and depressing to me. I no longer feel needed. I feel wanted as a wife, but not for the person I am inside. I want my husband to want me, not just a wife. I want to laugh and joke and poke fun at our issues, love with all of my heart without fear that what I've experienced in the past will show up in my experience again.

It's hard to move forward when your heart has been broken. I feel devalued. I am so much more than I am demonstrating and feeling. I want to be loved for whom I am inside, not a role I play and what is expected of me as the character playing that role. I don't feel like I'm being fully myself...I think I've already said that, but it deserves reiterating because that is what I truly feel. I feel as if I've been put on the back burner for so long that I'm coming to the end of my rope and beginning not to care.

I haven't been dancing in years. The last time I went dancing was when we took a Caribbean cruise and I wanted to check out a salsa dance lesson in one of the ballrooms. I went alone because he didn't want to go. I danced with some other ladies whose significant others didn't want to be involved either. I love to dance. It makes me feel free. It's fun. I love to move my body to different rhythms and beats. It's like I can feel the music inside me and I move however the music dictates.

I've had a very challenging seven years out of the last thirteen years although the full thirteen were spent starting and running my own personal training studio. The last seven years was when I finally decided what I wanted to study in school and began to seriously pursue my bachelor's degree. During the last three years, although I could really say it was easily maybe the last five years of school, I began to feel exhausted. By the time we took the cruise, I was in dire need of some rest, relaxation, and fun. I didn't get either of the three. Our time during that vacation was stressful. We were tired and stressed, which is why we needed a vacation, but I don't think it was relaxing or fun for either of us.

I was more stressed when we arrived back home because of my experiences during the cruise. I had, what I thought was, sinus challenges that later was diagnosed as acid reflux from all of the stress I was under, not to mention at that time eating anything and everything I thought I wanted. I can remember having lemonade and acidic fruits and food with lots of garlic and onions and chocolate chip cookies and chocolate cake and anything else that causes excess acid to be released in my stomach. I had no idea at the time that it was causing all of the coughing. I had a hard time sleeping even though I was using Musinex and Airborne the whole time we were on the weeklong cruise.

My mom also went on the cruise and she was having some health issues of her own, so I was a little worried about her, too. It was a complete wash as far as I'm concerned even though I tried to make the best of a bad situation. When we arrived back home I didn't feel as if I had been on vacation. All of the challenges I had before leaving I took with me, and then some. Feeling no relief, I had no choice but to jump back into my life and continue to work on completing school

I lost my voice for a week then developed pneumonia for about a month; thank God I was out of school for the summer by then. I had just gotten a Yorkie puppy; I've always wanted another dog. I had a dog as a child, but a car hit it, while I watched. For years, I wanted a replacement so that I could take better care of this one to make up for the last one. Well, I received her that year (2009) on the last day of the semester before summer. I had completed a presentation earlier that day that was half of my grade. I was taking depression medication by that time because the stress I was under caused me to begin feeling exhausted all of the time and in addition, I had started having anxiety episodes. I developed social anxiety and was unable to interact with my classmates at school. I couldn't drive and listen to the radio or drive and do anything else. It had become too much...I was burned out.

When I received Gracie (my Yorkie), I was at home alone all day with pneumonia and a puppy to take out, play with, feed, and try to house-train. I was coughing up pink stuff that I didn't realize was blood until the doctor told me. I didn't have an appetite. Each morning Gracie woke me up to take her out so we would go to the backyard because I couldn't walk too far. When I was done walking and feeding Gracie, I would take off my clothes and get back in bed. There was nothing else I could do. I had no energy. Since she was a puppy, she had to go out every couple of hours, so when she began making noise (her crate was in our bedroom), I would get up, put on my clothes, take her out to the backyard, bring her back in, and play with her for about 5 minutes, which was all I could take, put her back in her crate, and crawl back into bed until she woke me up again. This happened just about every two hours, so during the middle of the night and early morning hours, I would be outside with her or trying to get her to use the blue sheets we had for her to use. She didn't want anything to do with them, so I had no choice, but to take her out.

During these first few days of having her, I felt neglected. I was home alone all day, feeling terrible, no energy, and no support. I was so hurt and angry, I just started crying and I couldn't stop. I needed some relief so that I could get some rest in order to begin to start the healing process. I just wanted to make it clear how I felt at that time. When my husband arrived home, I told him how I felt through my tears and he finally said he understood and that he would take some time off work to help me. I told him I needed to go to the doctor, too and he took me. That's when I found out it was pneumonia. The doctor gave me an antibiotic and told me to eat because I had grown so weak that I could barely walk on my own. There was no way I was able to cook for myself; I didn't have the energy and found it hard to force myself to eat anyway. I had to force myself to eat canned soup and crackers and drink lots of water or tea. My ex cooked for me, but I was only able to eat a couple of bites of whatever was in front of me. I wanted to regain some strength back, so I ate what I could.

I didn't begin to feel better for at least a few weeks. I was still not completely healed after about three or four weeks. Having him home for a few days allowed me some time to rest while he took care of Gracie. Although I'm grateful for him deciding to do that, why did I have to break down in order to get some assistance? The pain of that experience is still with me even though I've physically moved on.

I was miserable in my marriage I'm sorry to say. I never thought I would ever believe or feel that way about us, but there it is. I felt misunderstood, unappreciated, and pushed to my absolute limits emotionally. On the way to my last class of the semester in which my team was scheduled to complete a final presentation, which was half of our grade (I didn't really say anything because of the social anxiety, but I had completed my portion of the work and had to at least show up), I received a call informing me that my mother-in-law (at the time) had been taken to the emergency room that morning for what the family thought was a stroke. Even though my husband and I were not getting along, I still wanted to be at the hospital with the family for support, but I also needed to be there for the presentation. He told me to do my presentation and he would keep me posted on her condition. So, I completed my presentation with my mother-in-law in the back of my mind...praying for the best outcome, but afraid of the worst.

At one point I couldn't even think. I had lost my short-term memory. I literally could not remember things right after I had done them and had no running dialogue in my head. There was no background noise. It was peaceful, but scary. I felt like I had broken my brain. I started taking the medication shortly after that and didn't feel like it had begun working yet. It had to be during the summer because if I had been going to classes at that time, I wouldn't have been able to keep up.

I had already felt the effects of the stress decreasing my mental abilities. I couldn't get anything over a B on any quiz or test at that time, when I had been an A student previously. I had even contemplated taking some time off because I didn't think I would be able to keep up, but I realized if the highest grade I could earn was a B, why stop going? It's not like I was so far gone that I would fail any of my classes. I just couldn't retain some of the information. I studied the way I always had, but missed many questions on quizzes and exams that I thought I knew. I was always surprised at the grade I would receive because I believed I had retained more than the results showed. I spoke with my instructors to let them know I had been diagnosed with significant depression, but that I was on medication and I would still endeavor to do the best I could. I didn't want to make any excuses for my state of being, but it was what it was and I wanted to be real, face it, be proactive, and do the best I could not to let it stop me from accomplishing my goal.

I didn't feel like I received much emotional support from the people I expected it from. I told very few people about my diagnosis, so I felt like I went through the whole experience by myself. My ex was here...still working...still coming home, but we weren't really connected anymore. We were mentally, emotionally, and spiritually disconnected. Maybe he didn't know what to do. I don't know if he thought I was faking it all or something else.

I think about those times. I felt like I was alone when I needed someone the most. I guess it goes back to expectations. I was disappointed when I didn't get what I expected, but was I expecting too much?

My Liberation from Denial

As stated previously, childhood is where my denials began. As an adult, I had to forgive myself for forgetting that I am important. I had to make sure that I was healthy and strong—mentally, physically, and emotionally, so that I could feel good and live well.

I had begun to think about everybody else's needs, wants, and expectations and put them before my own. I lost my perspective. I no longer knew what I wanted or needed. I was unsure of who I was and what I wanted for my life and myself.

I had to forgive myself for dragging my body and mind into my chamber of denials resulting in physical ailments. I had to apologize to my body for betraying it by not eating nutritious meals and exercising appropriately...even though I had a career as a personal fitness trainer and knew better. I had to forgive myself for allowing myself to get to the point where I began experiencing anxiety attacks because of all of the stress I created.

Even though I thought I was taking care of myself, in reality I wasn't. How could I be healthy and well, knowing something bizarre is happening within me, exhibiting low self-esteem, sadness, and anger most of the time, while experiencing physical ailments?

These are contradictions. I forgot there are mental and emotional components that make up my humanness. Most of the time I disassociated my mind from my body and focused only on my body staying healthy. How can my body stay healthy if my mind isn't?

I now understand when I take care of myself, and I am present in my life as an authentic being and not a caricature living in denial, I have high self-esteem. I am also healthy in mind and body, confident, beautiful, open, and free to be myself in any setting and with anyone.

Question(s):

- What are the issues that keep you stuck in denial?

- Write them down. No one has to see them but you.

Something to Live for: Poem

What is your something to live for?
In the midst of the season of depression,
Mine was a Yorkie named Gracie.
I named her Gracie because of God's Grace in my life.
She has been a saving grace for me in many ways.
She came exactly when I needed her most.
Always on time, they say.
There were many days I only left my bed
To care for her.
<u>Most</u> days during that time
I only got out of bed in the morning
Because she needed to go outside.
I can still see her as a little black and brown puppy,
Jumping across her crate from one side
To the other signaling to me
That she had to go out, really badly.
She is still my buddy when my way gets dark.
She's the dog I've always wanted.

I believe she came here just for me.

What is your something to live for?
Do you have something to live for?
There are too many things in this world
To be, do, have, see, learn, buy, rent, own, plan for,
Train for, feel, encounter, enjoy...Love;
Not having something to live for
Is just an excuse given to you by Deny!
She is mistaken.
See your Truth in my words and
Find your something to live for, today!

- Angela Taylor

"Those who cannot change their minds
cannot change anything."
- George Bernard Shaw

Chapter 12
Change It!

If there is something you don't like about yourself, decide what you want to change, discover the best way to go about changing it, plan the steps you will take, and begin to make change happen, one step at a time. You may be surprised at the opportunities open to you once you make up your mind to change.

I was shy as a child. I didn't want to be; I wanted to be popular and have lots of friends to do fun and exciting things with, but that wasn't my reality. I wanted to one day be an effective leader, but being too shy to speak up, even for myself, wasn't a characteristic of an effective leader. I didn't know my shyness was a symptom of low self-esteem until I was an adult in my late twenties. I didn't know what to do about it. I felt that my self-esteem was pretty high, but when I thought about it, I had doubts. I questioned whether I was good enough, smart enough, pretty enough, etc. Those thoughts were there for as far back as I can remember. I assumed the image of someone who had it all together and was well adjusted and self-assured, but inside I felt like dirt.

I came to realize (reluctantly) that because I felt this way (and told myself this often), I treated myself as such, and everyone else, too. I also realized I had been trying to force the people around me to be and do what I thought made me ok. I thought if they just behaved this way and talked to me that way, I would feel better and all would be well. These were denials. I came to understand that I couldn't do anything to change people for me to feel better. I had tried for many years and it hadn't worked yet, so who else in the relationship is there to change? Me. I had to change.

In order for me to change, I had to stop denying what was now plain to see. I'm the only person I can change. So, I took a step back, listened and observed as I interacted with people and became aware of the patterns we created. I saw each person as an individual, separate from our relationship (whatever the condition) and came to the conclusion that the issues I had with my relationships was about me. I tried to control the relationships and mold the people to fit what I thought I needed in my life instead of letting people be themselves and enjoying them as they were or leaving them alone. So, that is what I did. I enjoyed the relationships with the people I felt a positive mutual connection with and left the others alone. My life and I became better for it!

Change is Possible

I know there are naysayers that believe no one can change, but according to science, and many successful examples of people changing their lives for the better, CHANGE IS POSSIBLE!

People who tell you it's impossible to change more than likely haven't made the effort or tried, failed, and at some point gave up, whatever the reason. Their lives will show the results of their efforts. I'll show you later that change is absolutely possible, but challenging. I know because I felt like I was in hell before I decided I had to make changes or continue to die a slow death. Even feeling as if I was dying a slow death, didn't make me change until I got fed up with being sad and angry all of the time. I wanted my joy back. I didn't want to live the rest of my life miserable. I thought, "What is the point in living, if I'm miserable every day?" I had to make a change because I wanted to feel good. I wanted to be free. I wanted to have peace of mind. I wanted a new life...the life I've always dreamed of having. I thought, *if others can have it, why can't I? The only limits on my life are the ones I impose on myself.*

When we live our lives in denial, some of us pass away without living fully. By living fully, I mean we get to do, be, and live the way we would like to. I know some of you are saying, "Well, not everyone is supposed to live the life they want to." You say, "Luck only applies to rich people; people with influence; people with money; people with power; people of another race, culture, or religion, or maybe people who are underhanded and lie, cheat, and steal to get what they want." Well, ask anyone who is living their dream how they were able to do it, and you will get many different answers, but one thing they all have in common is that when faced with circumstances that seemingly stood in the way of them achieving their goal, they didn't deny what was staring them in the face. They became aware of it, acknowledged it, and chose to find out how to go beyond it or move through it. They asked for help when they needed it, gained more knowledge by going back to school or seeking a mentor, taking seminars, etc. Once you make up your mind to make change happen, nothing can stop you unless you let it. They say, when you really want to do something, you find a way to do it. Think about that for a moment. Is that true for you? Do you usually find a way to do what you really want to do and make excuses for the things you don't really want to do such as, "I'll do that later, when I'm not so busy"?

We Are the Original

Self-esteem building begins with love and forgiveness. We love ourselves by acknowledging our truth...we are unique individuals by design. No one else can be who we are, even if they copy our behavior. No one else can bring to the world what we, as unique individuals, have to offer; even if they have the same skills, talents, and abilities we have even if they may work in the same field, profession, or industry.

We are extraordinary people who have had unique experiences interpreted and expressed in our own ways. Each of us hauls everything we have and everything we are to everything we do. We have our own personalities, attitudes, and behaviors that make us incomparable along with an exceptional perspective personal to us. If only we understood that. We would all stand tall knowing that there is absolutely no one who can bring what we have to any table. No matter how marvelous they believe they are or how much more they think they have or how much more brilliant they believe themselves to be, they still cannot be us. We need to own that as individuals and decide we are going to make a difference with what we have to offer. We all know it is a compliment to have someone copy what we do, but we also have to understand they can never be the originals. For example, Michael Jackson, Whitney Houston, and Luther Vandross were people who used their talents to the best of their abilities and became household names and legends in their own time.

What dish did you bring to share at the table of life? Are you using all of the ingredients you were born with or underestimating the greatness waiting to be revealed? Are you telling yourself you don't have what it takes to make it?

The three people I mentioned, and many more like them who are still here with us, (Aretha Franklin, Tina Turner, Stevie Wonder, Jennifer Hudson, Mary J. Blige, and even Beyoncé) had people tell them they were lacking something that would hold them back (I know they are all musical entertainers, but I'm listening to music while writing and these are the names that were off the top of my head). Naysayers always tell those who are up and coming what they can't do. It didn't stop them or anyone else from rising to the top to be successful. Why should it stop you? The circumstances don't dictate to you what your opportunities will be. Opportunities open to you when you have developed, planned, learned, earned, and acquired what it takes to walk through the door.

Question:

- What can you do today to make a small change in the direction you want to go?

Revealing Opportunities Hidden by Denial

Living in denial can slow progress or stop progress altogether. When we are in denial about something, the denial story keeps us locked into the story. We begin to live the story that is only in our mind. We cease to be free, authentic, and progress in the areas of life where the stories are in play because Deny has us in a holding pattern. We are unable to move beyond where we are because in order to move forward, we need to acknowledge our truth. If we are in denial, we are hiding our truth. We have rendered ourselves unconscious in this area and move through our lives on automatic pilot. When this happens, we may look up one day and wonder what happened to the life we wanted. It's like when you are driving home from work and the whole time you are on the road, your mind is on something other than driving and before you know it, you are home, but you have no recollection of the trip. Your conscious mind is driving home while your subconscious mind and emotions may be at home already arguing with your spouse or children about something that happened this morning before you left for work. That happens every day we live in denial. The story becomes our focus. We think constantly about keeping something hidden, monitoring our actions and our conversations as to not give anything away. The problem is this increases our stress levels. Our mind is so consumed with the stories there is little energy left for ideas, inspiration, considering other perspectives, or alternatives. Those things may take time to occur to you or may not enter your thought process in that particular area because your mind is busy trying to keep the denial story alive.

Question(s):

- Why do you want to change?

- What good things will you experience once you have made the necessary changes?

- How will your life be different than it is now?

- What is the ultimate purpose/goal you want to achieve by implementing change?

- What will be your legacy?

- What do you believe is your purpose, right now?

- What do you expect to achieve in the future?

To Be Free: Poem

Ahhh, to be free!

Me, free—

Seems like I've been waiting forever

And finally I am here!

Basking in my own glow,

Radiating me, light and easy

Calm and clear.

It feels so good!

The goodness flows through my entire being!

There's nothing like it!

My mind is free of tangles and snares.

My body is energized, pain free, and well.

My relationships are harmonious and loving.

My lifestyle is comfortable, simple, and adventurous.

My spirit is in flight all around the core of me,

Suspended in open atmosphere,

Electrifying all that it touches,

And it touches everything.

Ahhh, to be free!

This is new to me, but I wouldn't trade it for anything.

Life just feels fresher.

Challenges have meaning;

Waves of light

Outpouring and inflowing.

Ahhh, to be free!

It doesn't matter how long it took me.

I am complete!

This is the way life was meant to be!

- Angela Taylor

Chapter 13

My 30 Steps Out of Denial

I have made a list based on how I began to move through my own denials. The order that I used is different than that listed in the 30-Steps Companion Guide and also the 31 Days for Overcoming Denial Day Book. Depending on where you are in your self-analysis, the order may also be different for you;

however, recording your thoughts in the Day Book and having them all contained in one place for you to look at them, go through the steps, and make sure **all** the steps have been completed before moving on to the next level could prove beneficial.

During the process of investigating my inner dialogue, I:

1. Examined my life in its current state.
2. Determined what was keeping my life feeling chaotic and uncomfortable and keeping me sad.
3. I discovered and uncovered my denial stories... faced reality...acknowledged my truth.
4. Thought about what I was avoiding.
5. Considered the benefits I received that kept me from making changes to my life.
6. Thought about what it would take for me to feel more authentic.
7. Thought about what I could do immediately to make my life feel more authentic.
8. Decided I needed help to get where I wanted to be.
9. Decided to seek a psychologist to help me unravel the ball of confusion in my mind.

10. Considered the negative and positive consequences of taking action.
11. Thought about my options, possibilities, and probabilities.
12. Allowed myself time to feel and express the emotions associated with the negative and positive consequences of taking action.
13. Determined if what I had to go through was worth feeling better, being better, and enjoying my life.
14. Decided I wanted to feel my best, be pain free (physically, mentally, and emotionally), and enjoy the rest of my life.
15. Examined my relationships and myself.
16. Decided I needed to forgive others in my life and myself.
17. Began writing in my journal...again.
18. Started writing down the things I was grateful for in my journal.
19. Became definite about what I wanted my life to look and feel like.
20. Decided what the best course of action would be for me to begin to feel better and make progress.
21. Determined the steps I needed to take to increase my joy and improve my life.

22. Planned my course of action (steps to take) to begin my life makeover.

23. Began meditating again to reduce stress (later began a different form of meditation in order to reconnect mentally and become aware spiritually of my connection with the Creator).

24. Began monitoring the emotions attached to the denial stories I told myself.

25. Began visualizing the future I desired, every day.

26. Began practicing new thoughts and stories to change my default programming.

27. Began reciting affirmations to help change my negative self-talk.

28. Began reading self-help and inspirational books that edified me intellectually as well as spiritually.

29. Became more active and added joy to my life by dancing for fun and exercise, riding my bike, and also walking my dog along the beautiful shores of Lake Michigan.

30. Recruited trusted loved ones to support me during my restoration process.

Notes About Therapy

I needed to discuss my current challenges and my past hurts with a person who would listen objectively without judgment (this is when I began to heal). I wanted to talk with someone I could trust to keep my private conversations to her. I needed someone who would be impartial and had years of experience counseling others professionally. I needed someone who had sound and effective advice because I wanted to see growth and progress. I needed a professional who knew how to handle my situation. I knew a psychologist/ psychiatrist could assist me in untangling my current situation, help me to discover answers to questions nagging at me since childhood, and put a name on what I was feeling (she diagnosed me with severe depression). This gave me a sense of relief because I knew what I was dealing with by enlisting my therapist's guidance, thus, I could begin the process leading me back to peace and a feeling of wholeness and freedom. My psychologist and psychiatrist helped me to look at situations and my relationships from a different perspective. They helped me to feel validated, confirmed answers hiding beneath my denial stories, and in addition, I was able to unload the years of pinned up negative energy in their offices, which freed my mind and helped to release excess negative energy. Talking about my past and my thoughts and feelings about the events and situations I found myself in gave me the space I needed to begin to think about other things. I began to ask myself the questions that would ultimately lead to my mental, physical, and emotional restoration and back to optimal health and wellness.

Notes About Medication

I don't like medication and didn't want to take it, but given my previous mental and emotional state and the fact I was still working through the situations that contributed to my depression and, at the time, I was in college completing my degree, I thought it was best for me to continue taking it, but only planned to use it until my doctor and I believed I didn't need it anymore. At the time I am writing this book, my medication has been decreased and I can see the day when I will no longer need it.

Therapy and/or medication may not be the answers for you; however, if you believe one or both may help, especially if you suspect you may be depressed, find a professional therapist to help you right away. Please do not wait until you get to the point of no return. There are also many alternative forms of therapy that are available. Seek the form of assistance that is best for you.

Perfection: Poem

I am perfect this way.

I need nothing to make me complete.

I was born complete.

Nothing can make me more.

I am already more different than anyone else.

Nothing can make me beautiful.

I was born beautiful!

I am told everyday how this and that can make me into
Something better.

How can that be, when I am already greater than that?

Why should I change my perfection?

To become a perception of someone else's definition?

What makes them right and God wrong?

It seems pretty arrogant to me for them

To assume a role that is already taken

By the One who created Everything,

Including them, and stated, "It Is Good."

I was good before I was born.

I am good now and

I predict nothing but good for my future!

I exude perfection from my pores

It fills my whole being inside and out!

It's not my fault they can't see the reality covered by the

Layers upon layers of illusions deceiving and haunting

Them like ghosts tainting their minds,

Spreading fear in the atmosphere.

They believe the lies that have been

Programmed into the system.

They have bought into the madness.

I have not!

Don't try to taint the reality of me.
I see beyond the nonsense society
Has been breastfed on for millennia,
Twisting our minds, until we conform.
I'm not conforming to anything that tells
Me I need to change the color of my skin,
The texture or color of my hair,
Shape of my eyes,
Length of my feet,
Contours of my nose,
Thickness of my lips,
Or the size of my breasts
To be received well by people who can only accept what
They are told is good by society's standards...those who
Only remain relevant in their own eyes because of a
Superficiality overdose. They are choking on the bits and
Pieces of regurgitated poison and believe it is a health
Promoting, wealth building, and image enhancing elixir.
All the while, the person they were born to become
Slowly dies a little every time the poison is ingested.

My perfection was born into chaos.
The chaos is not who or what I am.

I wear it like armor, placed upon me by others who wear
Their chaos proudly.
The armor is full of holes dented and scarred from
battles fought prior to my existence—hand-me-downs
that were not maintained well. The armor has been
Used, abused, and bequeathed to me.
To protect myself from harm, I have added metal plates
And patches of steel, disguised as education
To cover the places frayed and thin.

Perfection is reflected in the warmth or our smile.
Perfection is reflected in the empathy we show others.
Perfection is reflected in the kind words we speak.
Perfection is reflected in the actions we take to assist.
Perfection is reflected in our lifestyle.
Perfection indwells us every moment of each day.
We cannot become perfect.
We are perfect in our undiluted, non-polluted, pure state
of LOVE!

- Angela Taylor

"Reflect upon your present blessings, of which every man has many; not on your past misfortunes, of which all men have some."
- Charles Dickens

Chapter 14

Inspiration, Regeneration, Restoration

These are the ministries, books, and film genres that helped me the most during my regeneration at the lowest moments. I have an extended list of books under "Suggested Reading" of which helped me during my restoration when I began to see the light shining at the end of the tunnel that seemed to be filled with swirls of thick smoke.

Ministries

- **Bishop T. D. Jakes Ministries**: The Potter's House of Dallas, Texas
- **Joyce Meyer Ministries**: Christian non-profit organization based in Fenton, Missouri
- **Joel Osteen Ministries**: Lakewood Church of Houston, Texas

Books

- *Just Ask the Universe: A No-Nonsense Guide to Manifesting Your Dreams*, Michael Samuels. Michael Samuels, 2011
- *Let it Go: Forgive So You Can Be Forgiven*, Bishop T.D. Jakes. Atria Books, 2013
- *Reposition Yourself: Living Life Without Limits*, Bishop T.D. Jakes. Atria Books, 2008
- *The Power of Your Subconscious Mind,* Joseph Murphy. Start Publishing, LLC., 2012
- *Living The Science of Mind*, Ernest Holmes. DeVorss & Company, 1997
- *The Untethered Soul: The Journey Beyond Yourself,* Michael Singer. New Harbinger Publications, Inc., 2007

My Restoration

While reading, *The Untethered Soul,* I began to practice feeling the emotions that came up with the stories in my head and just breathing. I felt like I was releasing the negative emotions from my body. When I did it the first night (before going to bed) it felt so good that I continued to release until I felt cleansed. Whenever I would feel a negative emotion during the day, I would not resist it, I would just breathe and release the negative energy. I began to feel lighter and less angry as the energy was released. I recommend reading *The Untethered Soul.*

When I read his book, *Breathe in God's Love & Light* and began meditating with Walter Beckley, I felt a release of energy I had never felt before. I felt this energy swirling around in my body, especially my chest. It was like electricity. I almost couldn't handle it. Imagine sticking your finger in an electrical socket; that is what I imagine it would feel like. Not so intense that it would kill you, but intense enough to feel it and not be able to stop your body from moving because of its flow. I had never felt anything quite like this before. My eyes began to water and continued for a while as if my body was releasing something. I felt a connection on a very basic, yet dynamic, level. This energy is always with me; in fact, it is me and is all around me. I am able to access it and feel it more deeply now by meditating using Walters "New Bliss Breathing Meditation." It is different than the exercise I performed from the *Untethered Soul* and any other meditation I have ever practiced.

The exercise in *The Untethered Soul* was an emotional releasing process. The "New Bliss" Breathing Meditation allowed me to: connect my body and mind with the energy that flows through everything, tap into the energy, increase its flow, bathe in it, and transcend all thought while connecting with a Source/Universal Mind/Superconscious Mind/Higher Power/God. There are no affirmations to listen to or recite; just connecting to the source of my energy and feeling it transform me from the inside out. For me, it feels like tapping into heaven.

Reading *Reposition Yourself* by Bishop T.D. Jakes, gave me hope when I had little. It inspired me when I felt like I was lost, stuck between where I was and where I wanted to be.

Reading *It Works if You Work It* by the late, great Reverend Doctor Johnnie Colemon, reminded me to use the principles I grew up learning about in my daily life.

Conversing with my mom, Reverend Constance Taylor, and tapping into her vast bank vault of knowledge and wisdom helped me to feel connected, uplifted, spiritually edified, and loved. Thanks mom!

Activities that help to change my default settings, increased my activity level, released excess weight, increased my energy level, and increased my enjoyment of life. Some of these activities consisted of:

- Exercising
- Reading
- Writing in my journal
- Dancing
- Listening to music
- Meditating ("New Bliss" breathing meditation)
- Praying
- Practicing changing my default programming
- Reciting affirmations to help change my negative self-talk
- Imaging my future life
- Practicing being in the moment
- Watching romantic comedies
- Watching stand-up comedies
- Playing with my dog, Gracie
- Walking along the shores of Lake Michigan

- Experimenting with fruit smoothie recipes
- Riding my bike

Notice all of the activities are in the present tense; it is important for me to continue to do the things that keep me uplifted, active, and filled with joy and energy. When I stop, I notice stress and anxiety start to set in.

It is important to know even when we begin feeling better the activities and practices that allowed us to feel good must continue and become a part of our everyday lifestyle. Think of the goal of this process as a new lifestyle that supports you being healthy, happy, and well. It is not like a fad diet or cleanse you may do every once in a while when you feel like you need it. Your mindset is a healthy, happy lifestyle. **This is key!**

Come out of denial, so you can feel good, be healthy, and live a long, pain-free, joy-filled, harmonious, peaceful, love-infused, vital, intentional, proactive, drama-free, authentic, bountiful, and fulfilling life or at the very least get as close as you can to these wonderful states of being.

Wouldn't it be worth it to enjoy even a fraction of the opportunities that will become available to you?

Yes! Change Is Possible!

Thank you for reading my book. I hope that you read something that helps you begin to ask questions to uncover denial stories that may be controlling your life.

Suggested Reading

- *The T.D. Jakes Relationship Bible: Life Lessons on Relationships from the Inspired Word of God*, Bishop T.D. Jakes. Atria Books, 2008
- *New Brain, New World: How the Evolution of a New Human Brain Can Transform Consciousness and Create a New World*, Erik Hoffman. Hay House, 2012
- *The Power of Perception: 6 Steps to Behavior Change*, Hyrum W. Smith. Juxtabook Digital Marketing, Inc. 2013
- *Subliminal: How Your Unconscious Mind Rules Your Behavior*, Leonard Mlodinow. Vintage, 2013
- *Frequency: The Power of Personal Vibration*, Penney Peirce. Atria Books/Beyond Words, 2011

- *The Millionaire Mind*, Thomas J. Stanley Ph.D. (Electronic edition) Rosetta- Books, 2001

- *To Believe or not to Believe: The Social and Neurological Consequences of Belief Systems*, Rahasya Poe. Xlibris, 2009

- *Ten Interesting Things About Human Behavior*, Suzanne L. Davis. MindGame Books, 2012-2013

- *Overcoming Depression: How to Recognize, Understand and Overcome Depression and Anxiety Naturally*, Daniel Hall. Amazon, 2013

- *The Gifts of Imperfection: Let Go of Who You Think You Should Be and Embrace Who You Are*, Brene Brown. Hazelden, 2010

- *Quantum Enigma: Physics Encounters Consciousness,* Bruce Rosenblum and Fred Kuttner. Oxford University Press, 2011

- *The Prospering Power of Love*, Catherine Ponder. DeVorss & Company, 2006

- *The Biology of Belief: Unleashing the Power of Consciousness, Matter & Miracles*, Bruce H. Lipton, Ph.D. Hay House, Inc., 2008

- *The Instinct to Heal: Curing Depression, Anxiety, and Stress without Drugs and Without Talk*

Therapy, David Servan-Schreiber, M.D., Ph.D., Rodale Books, 2005

- *The Honeymoon Effect: The Science of Creating Heaven on Earth*, Bruce H. Lipton, Ph.D. Hay House, 2013

- *I Thought it Was Just Me (But it isn't): Women Reclaiming Power and Courage in a Culture of Shame*, Brene Brown. Penguin Group, Inc., 2007

- *Why Quantum Physicists Do Not Fail: Learn the Secrets of Achieving Almost Anything Your Heart Desires*, Greg Kuhn. Createspace Independent Publication Platform, 2012

- *Breathe in God's Love & Light,* Walter L. Beckley. Radiant Living Publishing, 2012

- *A Life Worth Living: Focusing on What Really Matters*, Geri Laing. Discipleship Publications International, 2005

- *Ask and it is Given: Learning to Manifest Your Dreams,* Esther and Jerry Hicks (Abraham Teachings). Hay House, 2004

- *The Vortex: Where the Law of Attraction Assembles All Cooperative Relationships*, Esther and Jerry Hicks (Abraham Teachings). Hay House, 2009

- *The Amazing Power of Deliberate Intent: Living the Art of Allowing*, Esther and Jerry Hicks (Abraham Teachings). Hay House, 2006

- *E-Squared: Nine Do-it-Yourself Energy Experiments that Prove Your Thoughts Create Your Reality*, Pam Grout. Hay House, 2012

- *The I of the Storm: Embracing Conflict, Creating Peace*, Gary Simmons. Unity House, 2001

- *You Can Heal Your Life*, Louise Hay. Hay House, 1999

- *The Secret*, Rhonda Byrne. Atria Books/Beyond Words, 2010

- *The Four Agreements: A Practical Guide to Personal Freedom (A Toltec Wisdom Book, Book 1)*, Don Miguel Ruiz and Janet Mills. Amber-Allen Publishing, 1997

- *The Mastery of Love: A Practical Guide to the Art of Relationship (A Toltec Wisdom Book)*, Don Miguel Ruiz and Janet Mills. Amber-Allen Publishing, 2011

- *The Power of Now: A Guide to Spiritual Enlightenment*, Eckhart Tolle. Namaste Publishing, 2004

- *A New Earth: Awakening to Your Life's Purpose,* Eckhart Tolle. Plume, 2008

- *Coming to Our Senses: Healing Ourselves and the World Through Mindfulness,* Jon Kabat-Zinn. Hachette Books, 2006

- *The Book of Awakening: Having the Life You Want by Being Present to the Life You Have,* Michael Singer. Conari Press, 2011

- *The Success Principles: How to Get from Where You Are to Where You Want to Be,* Jack Canfield with Janet Switzer. William Morrow Paperbacks, 2006

- *It Works If You Work It: Lesson Sermons from the Pulpit,* Reverend Johnnie Colemon, D.D., D.H.L.

- *Reverend Ike's Secrets for Health, Joy, and Prosperity for You: A Science of Living Study Guide,* Reverend Frederick Eikerenkoetter Th.B., D.Sc.L., PhD. (Reverend Ike).

- *Why Do I Do That? Psychological Defense Mechanisms and the Hidden Ways They Shape Our Lives,* Joseph Burgo, PhD. New Rise Press, 2012

My Sunflower: Poem

It all began with a conscious question

My subconscious already knew the answer to.

She hid it behind her wall of glass

Secured for a good while I must say.

Every now and then I would catch a glimpse

As if peeking through a stained glass window Speckled

by cascading beads of rain

Gliding down to the wood frame

And dripping to the ground below.

A quick flash of colors and emotion,

Then I would resume my day.

Soon I gave her permission to

Bring my inquiry closer,

For a more thorough observation.

 I wanted to explore the mystery of it.

As it came nearer still

And I pressed my nose against the glass,

I decided to step back

And give the glass a more careful examination.

I found that in addition to color,

It had tint and shadow added to the mold of it.

I asked my subconscious to remove the glass

And found that the shapes and colors

Were those of a sunflower opening to full bloom,

Activated by a bright light and gentle breeze,

Which embraced me,

As if greeting me with a big hug.

I squinted and studied the scene,

Not believing my eyes.

The thing I was so afraid to see,

Was a marvel to witness.

I had never seen a sunflower such as this.

The outermost petals were yellow

Like I've seen many times before,

But moving toward the center,

The petals growing smaller and more

Narrow were a variety of shades of yellow,

From pale yellow to burnt orange.

As this extraordinary natural wonder opened,

I could see the center, which was

Even more breathtaking,

Colors moving from bright red,

To brown, and back to pale yellow in the center.

I asked my subconscious

If this was all there was

Behind the glass the whole time.

She said, "Yes, you could have viewed it

At any moment, but

You weren't sure what you would find,

So I kept it hidden until you were ready."

I asked her the significance of the glass

And she said,

"The appearance of the glass

Is forever changing as you gain more wisdom

And begin to see things as they truly are."

I laughed and said,

"I guess I have a lot more to learn."

She smiled and nodded ever so slightly.

- Angela Taylor

Sources

Websites

Carey, Benedict. (2007). Denial Makes the World Go Round. Nytimes.com. Retrieved on June 10, 2015, from (http://www.nytimes.com/2007/health/research/20deni.html).

Grohol, J. Psy.D. (2013). Denial is a Powerful Impediment to Treatment. *Psych Central*. Retrieved on September 29, 2015, from http://psychcentral.com/lib/denial-is-a-powerful-impediment-to-treatment/

Kubler-Ross, E. (n.d.). On Death and Dying: What the Dying have to teach Doctors, Nurses, Clergy, and Their Families. Retrieved June 10, 2015, from http://www.ekrfoundation.org/five-stages-of-grief/.

Mayo Clinic Staff. (2004). Denial: When it helps, When it Hurts. Mayoclinic.org. Retrieved June 10, 2015, http://www.mayoclinic.org/healthy-lifestyle/adult-health/in-depth/denial/art-20047926?pg=1

Online References

Denial. *ABC Thesaurus online*. In ABC Thesaurus. Retrieved June 10, 2015, from http://www.thesaurus.com/browse/denial?s=t.

Denial. [Def (6)]. (n.d.). *Merriam-Webster online.* In Merriam-Webster. Retrieved June 10, 2015, from http://www.merriam-webster.com/dictionary/denial.

Depression. *ABC Thesaurus online.* In ABC Thesaurus. Retrieved June 10, 2015, from http://www.thesaurus.com/browse/depression?s=t.

Depression. [Def. 2b (1)]. (n.d.). *Merriam-Webster online.* In Merriam-Webster. Retrieved June 10, 2015, from http://www.merriam-webster.com/dictionary/depression.

Mantra. [Def. 2]. (n.d.). *Merriam-Webster online.* In Merriam- Webster. Retrieved June 23, 2015, from http://www.merriam-webster.com/dictionary/mantra.

Mess. [Def. 3, 3a]. (n.d.). *Merriam-Webster online.* In Merriam-Webster. Retrieved June 23, 2015, from http://www.merriam-webster.com/dictionary/mess.

Books

Beckley, Walter L. (2012) Breathe in God's Love & Light. *The 8 Areas of the Circle of Life.* Richton Park, Illinois: Radiant Living Publishing.

Burgo, Joseph, PhD. (2012). *Why Do I Do That: Psychological Defense Mechanisms And The Hidden Ways They Shape Our Lives* (Kindle ed.). Chapel Hill, North Carolina: New Rise Press.

Douglas, David. (2015). *Neuroplasticity: The Secret Behind Brain Plasticity (*Kindle ed.) Loco Media.

Halkin, Hillel M.D. (2013). *Telling Silences: A Doctor's Tales of Denial (*Kindle ed.) Amazon.

Hatfield PhD., R. (2013). *The Everything Guide to The Human Brain: Journey Through the Parts of the Brain, Discover How It Works, and Improve Your Brain's Health.* Avon, Massachusetts: Adams Media.

Shelton, C.D. (2013). *Brain Plasticity: Rethinking How the Brain Works* (Kindle ed.) Choice PH.

Singer, Michael A. (2007). *The Untethered Soul: The Journey Beyond Yourself.* Oakland California: New Harbinger Publications and Noetic Books.

The Holy Bible, The Precious Promises Edition. Lake Wylie, South Carolina: Christian Heritage (1988). Print.

About The Author

Angela Taylor was born and raised on the West side of Chicago. Her love for reading and writing began at an early age. She began recording her thoughts, experiences, poetry, short stories, and essays in her journals and has continued to do so throughout the years.

Angela is an ACE Certified Fitness Instructor and Personal Trainer. She is also a certified Zumba instructor and has taught various fitness classes in several fitness facilities in and around the Chicagoland area, including her alma mater the University of Illinois at Chicago. She started her own personal training business in which she led and directed fitness programs, boot camps, and conducted small group training and circuit classes. She also founded a walking club, in addition to training her individual fitness clients.

After graduating from the University of Illinois at Chicago with a bachelor's degree in kinesiology, Angela began chronicling her adventures (relationships, activities, changes in perception and behavior, mental and emotional states, epiphanies, understanding obtained by listening to people with knowledge and wisdom) and the many books she has read. During this time, she absorbed invaluable insight that helped her restore her body, mind, and life back to their natural healthy forms of being. Angela realized that once she stopped the cycle of denial controlling her life, she was free mentally and emotionally to begin making changes to her life that brought her back to authenticity. Acknowledging, examining, and unraveling the denial stories that kept her from moving beyond her present circumstances allowed her to uncover and take advantage of the opportunities available to her. It was then she began to feel better, release excess body fat, feel love, reclaim her energy, joy, and peace...and begin writing this book.

Angela still lives in the Chicago area collaborating with and enjoying her new love relationship; writing poetry, short stories and essays; walking with her Gracie; conducting fitness classes and fitness training and meeting and communicating with her readers as an author, speaker, and workshop presenter.

For additional information visit:

www.BeautyAndVanity.com

www.DenialAndDepression.com

or email Angela at:

Angela@BeautyAndVanity.com

contact@DenialAndDepression.com

www.ingramcontent.com/pod-product-compliance
Lightning Source LLC
Chambersburg PA
CBHW072100040426
42334CB00041B/1475